DINOSAURS

a Golden Guide® from St. Martin's Press

by
EUGENE S. GAFFNEY, Ph.D.
Curator of Vertebrate Paleontology,
American Museum of Natural History

St. Martin's Press New York

FOREWORD

This guide is intended to provide easy access to information about the best-known dinosaurs, those most likely to be encountered in North American museums. Along with skeletal drawings and reconstructions, it includes information on such subjects as evolution, locomotion, and feeding.

John Dawson has produced a lasting contribution to the popularization of fossils with his accurate and very beautiful renditions of extinct animals. Caroline Greenberg, Senior Editor, has kept this project together; her hard work and skill are responsible for its successful completion. Barbara and Karen Gaffney helped with the manuscript and provided moral support.

I am particularly indebted to my predecessors and colleagues at the American Museum of Natural History for creating and maintaining an incomparable collection of fossil vertebrates and an incomparable atmosphere for their study.

E.S.G.

CONTENTS

DINOSAURS

For the entire length of the Mesozoic Era, more than 150 million years, dinosaurs were the dominant type of four-legged animals. Dinosaurs were very successful, hundreds of different kinds evolved, and they lived in many different land habitats.

The word dinosaur means "terrible lizard" and was coined by a British scientist, Sir Richard Owen, in 1842. Fossil teeth and bones were being discovered that indicated a gigantic form of extinct animal. The popular idea of dinosaurs as gigantic, ill-adapted monsters isn't very different from what it was in Owen's day. But after more than 100 years of discovery and study, we now have more accurate ideas about

dinosaurs. Certainly most were gigantic and monstrous, but many were small and active, and some are still alive today as birds (p. 92). Dinosaurs were so well adapted that they survived for hundreds of millions of years and evolved a bewildering variety of structures. Although we know something about the forms of their skeletons and their evolutionary relationships, the behavior and biology of the extinct dinosaurs is an elusive topic prone to speculation and controversy. Trackways (pp. 40, 62), burial environments (pp. 14, 64), skin impressions (pp. 21, 116), fossils of juveniles (pp. 80, 123), and other sources provide clues to dinosaur habits, but unanswered questions greatly outnumber well-supported solutions.

DINOSAUR DISCOVERIES

Dinosaur bones had been found for hundreds or perhaps thousands of years before Sir Richard Owen named them. But as with so many aspects of the earth's natural history, information about dinosaurs came gradually and irregularly.

Emergence of critical attitudes in science in the 18th and 19th centuries prompted new ideas about fossils, and dinosaurs began feeding controversies about extinction and evolution. Such 19th-century paleontologists as Georges Cuvier, William Buckland, and Gideon Mantell promoted the idea of comparing fossils with recent animals. They observed that fossil limbs and teeth were similar to those of recent reptiles and mammals but that there were significant differences as well.

By the middle of the 19th century, fossils had provided evidence that vast groups of animals had become extinct and that these animals were similar in many ways to recent animals. Dinosaurs were interpreted as evidence that life evolved, or changed. Beginning in the second half of the 19th

Owen's original restoration of *Megalosaurus* in 1854 was based on only a few bones and was, therefore, inaccurate. *Megalosaurus* was later found to be very similar to *Allosaurus* (p. 76).

century, intensive efforts were undertaken to discover more specimens.

Sir Richard Owen's reconstructions of such dinosaurs as *Megalosaurus* were based on only a few bones and later required many changes. In Philadelphia, Joseph Leidy and Waterhouse Hawkins mounted the first dinosaur skeleton, *Hadrosaurus*, in 1868. Although they had more bones than Owen did, their skeleton was still incomplete. The real advance of knowledge about dinosaurs awaited the discovery of nearly complete and well-preserved specimens.

The dinosaur fields of western North America were discovered in the latter part of the 1800s, and other rich dinosaur finds were made in Central Asia, East Africa, and Europe. It was the western North American collections, however, unearthed in a period from about 1890 to 1920, that yielded most of the well-preserved dinosaur specimens known today.

A specimen of *Hadrosaurus* from New Jersey was more complete and provided the basis for the first mounted dinosaur skeleton. It was posed in a more lifelike upright posture, but there were still errors.

MORE EVIDENCE A breakthough came in 1878, when a rich deposit of the Early Cretaceous dinosaur *Iguanodon* was discovered in a Belgian coal mine. After great difficulties in collecting and preserving this material, the first mounted *Iguanodon* skeleton was exhibited in 1883. The final collection, exhibited in Brussels today, consists of 11 free-standing skeletons and 20 others mounted in their original positions.

The discovery of vast fossil fields in western North America soon eclipsed the Belgian finds and attracted Barnum Brown, the Sternberg family, Earl Douglass, and other legendary dinosaur hunters. The years 1900 to 1915 were the "golden age" of dinosaur collecting, resulting in finds that filled the great dinosaur halls of North America. These are the source of our current ideas about dinosaurs.

Below: Barnum Brown (right) and Jacob Wortman (left), early fossil hunters from the American Museum of Natural History, collecting *Apatosaurus* in the Como Bluff region of Wyoming in 1899. Facing page: Some of the more important dinosaur discoveries made in the early years of dinosaur work.

1889 *Triceratops*
Lance Creek, Wyoming

1878 *Iguanodon*
Bernissart,
Belgium

1877 *Apatosaurus*
Morrison, Colorado

Stegosaurus
Morrison, Colorado

1832 *Hylaeosaurus*
Tilgate Forest, England

1825 *Iguanodon*
Tilgate Forest, England

1824 *Megalosaurus*
Stonesfield, England

9

WHERE DINOSAURS HAVE BEEN FOUND

Most of the major dinosaur discoveries are shown on this map. The absence of dinosaurs in Antarctica may be due to poor exposures and difficulties of collection rather than to

actual absence of fossils. New discoveries of duck-billed dinosaurs and meat-eating dinosaurs in the North Slope of Alaska show that there is still a great potential for new localities that extend the range and the environment of dinosaurs.

GEOLOGIC TIME

The earth is probably 4 to 5 billion years old. Precisely when life first appeared on earth is not known, but the oldest fossils are more than 3 billion years old. The early fossil record of life is sparse, and fossils are not common until the beginning of the Cambrian Period about 600 million years ago. The first land vertebrates appeared in the Devonian Period about 410 million years ago. Dinosaurs and mammals both appeared as fossils at about the same time—in the Triassic Period about 250 million years ago. For the next 185 million years, dinosaurs flourished while the mammals remained inconspicuous. Mammals did not become greatly diversified until the extinction of the dinosaurs some 65 million years ago.

The time scale shown on the facing page is based on a combination of the following two methods of dating.

RADIOMETRIC DATING The rate of decay, or breakdown, of certain radioactive elements is constant, and by carefully measuring the products and comparing them with the remaining amount of the original element, the precise date of formation of the element can be accurately determined. However, radioactive elements are not common in fossil-bearing sediments. They are more common in volcanic or other igneous rocks.

CORRELATION of rocks in one place with rocks of the same age in another place is the second method of dating fossils. Though by far the most common method, this determines only relative rather than absolute age. Correlation is often done with fossils, based on the assumption that specimens of the same or closely related species lived at the same time. By using the principles of correlation, many fossil deposits that lack radioactive elements can be dated.

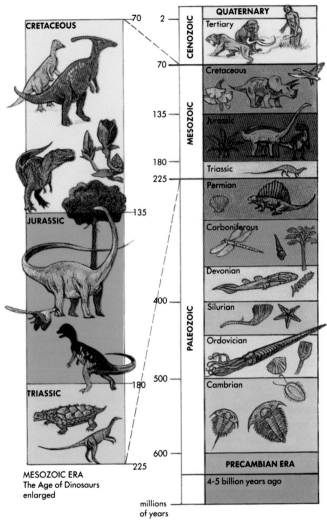

CRETACEOUS 70

JURASSIC 135

TRIASSIC 180

225

MESOZOIC ERA
The Age of Dinosaurs
enlarged

		QUATERNARY
CENOZOIC	2	Tertiary
	70	
MESOZOIC		Cretaceous
	135	Jurassic
	180	Triassic
	225	
PALEOZOIC		Permian
		Carboniferous
		Devonian
	400	Silurian
		Ordovician
	500	Cambrian
	600	
		PRECAMBIAN ERA
		4-5 billion years ago

millions
of years

13

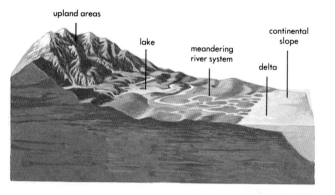

upland areas

lake

continental slope

meandering river system

delta

HOW DINOSAURS WERE PRESERVED

Dinosaurs and other animals we know only as fossils were buried and preserved by natural processes, then later exposed and found. Most well-preserved dinosaur fossils are found in what were large river systems, similar to the present-day delta region of the Mississippi River.

Large rivers carry great quantities of mud and sand, eroded from uplands. Much of the mud and sand is deposited offshore, but large amounts are also deposited on the banks of the river system as it forms branches and meanders back and forth.

Animals living in the flood plain may fall into the river during times of flooding. Sometimes skin imprints are left, but the soft tissues rot, leaving the bones buried in the mud or sand. Minerals may invade the bone cell spaces, or the entire bone may be replaced. Later, uplifts or mountain building raise the now-consolidated sandstone or shale so that erosion by wind and water removes the old sediment. Parts of the skeleton are then exposed and become visible to the lucky collector.

1. Death of animal in or near an area that has rapid deposition of sand or mud, like a river

2. Soft tissues rot away. Skin imprints may be formed if the deposition is very rapid.

3. Burial by sand or mud

4. Mineralization of bones by dissolved chemicals in ground water

5. Uplift of rocks containing fossils, and erosion, expose bones.

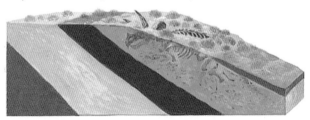

COLLECTING DINOSAURS

Fossil hunters begin looking where there are lots of exposures of rocks old enough to contain dinosaurs. Fossil bones are usually found when fragments are seen scattered on the surface of the ground. Rarely do fossil hunters go to a place and start digging before seeing an exposed bone.

The extent of the bone or skeleton is determined by using small picks and shovels. Usually there is only one bone or a part of a bone. Seldom found are connected, or articulated, bones or a partial or complete skeleton. Even more rarely are many skeletons found.

Bone surfaces are generally frag-mentary and need to have dilute glue, shellac, or resin painted over them. At this stage bones may be covered with moistened tissue or newspaper to fit into cracks and spaces. This is the most time-consuming part of collecting fossils and requires the most skill.

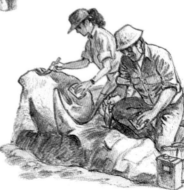

Cracks make it possible to divide the skeleton or bone into manageable units. These units are further separated by trenching; some undercutting may also be done. Each unit can then be wrapped, using plaster-soaked cloth or plaster bandages. The bone is usually protected from the plaster by newspaper.

The plaster bandages are wrapped around the blocks as tightly as possible and are also placed on top. When completely set and hardened, the block is further undercut and finally turned over. If the job is successful, no bone sticks out of the bottom, and nothing falls out.

Blocks are left as is or are wrapped completely in plaster bandages, cloth tape, or rope for shipment to the preparation laboratory. Very hard rock, very soft rock, thick overlying rock, or water can make these simple tasks nearly impossible. Rocksaws, jackhammers, backhoes, bulldozers, and other tools can help, but too little money and too much isolation may prevent their use.

EXHIBITING DINOSAURS

Dinosaur skeletons are great attractions in natural history museums. Some of the earliest were mounted even though they were relatively incomplete, but the majority of specimens now in major museums are nearly whole skeletons.

In early mounts, metal pipes were used to support the great weight. The metal was bent and contoured to fit the bones as inconspicuously as possible. In panel mounts, the skeleton was embedded in a mesh or frame covered by plaster. Today a common trend is to exhibit high-quality fiberglass and plastic casts of skeletons. Such casts allow museums to put together a large hall of dinosaurs even when they have few actual specimens of dinosaurs of their own. Unfortunately, this trend deprives the public of new, real specimens, an essential ingredient in keeping the science healthy.

Mounting one of the first large dinosaur skeletons, an *Iguanodon*, in 1880 in Belgium, completed and placed on exhibit in 1883.

Left: Preparing a *Styracosaurus* skeleton for mounting as a two-sided panel. See p. 140 for the completed mount.

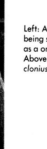

Left: A *Monoclonius* skeleton being set into a plaster base as a one-sided plaster mount. Above: The completed *Monoclonius* mount

WHAT DO WE REALLY KNOW ABOUT DINOSAURS?

There are various types of dinosaur fossils, but the most common is bone. Bone is made of stringlike protein fibers, collagen, that provide a network, or matrix, in which a hard mineral, apatite, is deposited. When an animal dies, the protein fibers decay and are lost. A fossil bone forms when the animal is buried by some natural event, such as mud or sand flowing over it in a stream. Although the collagen fibers are lost, the mineral is preserved, keeping the form and shape of the bone as it was. In a process not well understood, other minerals are usually added to the original apatite, filling in the spaces and making it heavier.

Because the process of burial usually damages bones and scatters them, complete skeletons with all the bones in their proper position are rare. Nonetheless, many skeletons have been found, and they form the main body of information about dinosaurs. Complete skeletons reveal a great deal about the size and shape of an animal, and leave little doubt about general features. Specimens have also been found in which skin and muscle imprints yield information about soft tissues. Very rarely, fine sediment buried a dinosaur before decay of the skin and muscles took place. Such specimens show the texture and form of the skin, and reveal that dinosaurs had a pebbly, patterned surface rather than overlapping scales, as in recent lizards and snakes.

A fossil bone usually contains the original mineral, apatite, plus other minerals that were added while the bone was buried in rock. The original microscopic structure is usually preserved.

This imprint of dinosaur skin was formed in mud, now hardened to rock. The original skin rotted away during burial.

The habitats of dinosaurs—whether they lived in swamps or grasslands, in forests or along beaches—cannot be determined directly from the location of a fossil skeleton. The only direct evidence a skeleton gives us about where the dinosaur once lived is the place of its burial, and animals are not always buried where they lived.

Dinosaur diet and locomotion are often better understood, but again, there is much speculation and little hard evidence. One specimen of a duck-billed dinosaur is known with stomach contents preserved (p. 126), but the diet of other dinosaurs must be guessed at by comparing their teeth and feeding mechanisms with recent reptiles and mammals in the hope that similar teeth are correlated with similar diets. Again, general ideas can be developed. For instance, sharp, pointed teeth usually indicate meat eaters. But we cannot tell from this feature alone whether the animal was a predator, or whether it was a scavenger, feeding on dead carcasses.

Skin color, vocal sounds, social behavior, migratory habits, and interaction between species are all subjects we would like to know something about. It is useful to make intelligent speculations about such matters and to examine the fossil record to test our ideas. But the nature of fossils imposes severe restrictions on the type of information that can be learned, and many interesting questions cannot be answered.

WERE DINOSAURS WARM-BLOODED?

The chemicals inside animals that produce all the reactions and processes necessary for life will only function within certain temperature limits. If an animal becomes too hot or too cold, it will die. Animals have evolved various mechanisms to maintain their temperature limits.

Living reptiles tend to control their temperature by modifying their behavior. They are commonly called "cold-blooded" because they depend on their surroundings for temperature control, and may become slow moving or inactive during cool spells.

Mammals and birds, on the other hand, tend to use chemical mechanisms to maintain optimum temperature — producing internal heat (and cooling) irrespective of outside temperatures. Mammals and birds are often called "warm-blooded" because of this.

However, the temperature adaptations of animals are extremely complex, and it is inaccurate to say that an animal is either completely "warm-blooded" or completely "cold-blooded."

Nevertheless, some paleontologists have argued that dinosaurs were "warm-blooded" like mammals and birds. Most of the evidence for this idea is related to the fact that the skeletons of dinosaurs have many features seen only in active and fast-moving animals. According to this argument, dinosaurs must have been "warm-blooded" in order to maintain high-activity levels. Additionally, microscopic studies of bones suggest that dinosaurs grew rapidly and possibly had high-activity levels. However, none of this evidence is capable of showing the difference between *permanent* high-activity levels, as seen in most mammals, and *temporary* high-activity levels, as seen in most living reptiles. Furthermore, few paleontologists would defend the contrary notion that dinosaurs were overgrown lizards.

At present we may draw the following conclusions:

1. Dinosaur temperature control was probably very complex, as in living animals. "Warm-blooded" versus "cold-blooded" means little, because it is too simple.

2. Dinosaurs probably did not have lizardlike temperature control.

3. Available evidence cannot show that dinosaurs had either a mammalian or an avian (bird) method of temperature control. Neither can it show that they did *not* have such mechanisms, or that they had a peculiarly dinosaurian method about which we know nothing.

No one knows whether or not all dinosaurs had permanent high-activity levels like mammals, but many dinosaurs were probably very active at least some of the time.

HOW ACCURATE ARE DINOSAUR RECONSTRUCTIONS?

Even with a complete, nicely articulated dinosaur skeleton with skin imprints, a wholly objective reconstruction of the living dinosaur isn't possible. Two assumptions must be made.

First, it is necessary to assume there are no problems with the skeleton and the degrees of movement of the articulated bones. In general, this isn't a serious difficulty, although it's been shown in recent years just how hard it is to choose among widely differing stances, tail postures, and even whether a dinosaur was bipedal, quadrupedal, or both. For example, some have argued that sauropods dragged their tails, while others have claimed the tails were held erect and could even be curled. Whether a ceratopsian had sprawling or erect forelimbs has been debated. In the absence of well-preserved specimens, the exact position of bones in the living animal is open to variable interpretations.

Secondly, the restoration of muscles requires the assumption that near relatives of dinosaurs, namely recent birds and crocodiles, have muscle patterns and attachments not very different from dinosaurs. This is difficult to test, because even the presence of muscle scars and attachments can be misleading when dealing with bones very different from the living model. Combining a "reasonable" amount of guesswork (something that differs widely among those who study dinosaurs) and a thorough knowledge of recent animals can result in a "best guess" reconstruction.

The most important thing to realize about dinosaur reconstructions is the vast separation between the reality of the actual bones and the speculations necessary for a fully fleshed and colored reconstruction. While it is important to give some idea of what dinosaurs *might* have looked like, these restorations cannot be considered "the truth."

The reconstruction of *Iguanodon* from the work of Dr. David Norman is the result of detailed comparisons between living animals and well-preserved dinosaur skeletons. No one will ever know if it is absolutely accurate, but it is a "best guess."

DINOSAUR DIMENSIONS

In 1962, E. H. Colbert made an estimate of dinosaur weights, using restored models. His results are listed on the facing page, with approximate lengths of known skeletons.

Colbert's estimates relied on two assumptions: 1. that dinosaurs had approximately the same specific gravity as modern crocodiles and other related animals, and 2. that the reconstructions used were accurate. While the first assumption is probably correct, the second may not be.

Colbert used models made over the years by different people. The resulting estimates are then only as accurate as the restorations. The problem is that no one actually knows how accurate any particular dinosaur restoration really is. Although these weights are probably not off by too much, it's difficult to determine the limits.

New discoveries of giant sauropods even larger than *Brachiosaurus* have led to speculations that some may have weighed more than 100 tons.

speculative reconstruction of
Ultrasaurus (possibly the same
as *Brachiosaurus*)

100 ft.

	estimated weight	approximate length
Theropods		
Compsognathus	8 lbs.	2 feet
Tyrannosaurus	7½ tons	47 feet
Allosaurus	2 tons	30 feet
Sauropods		
Diplodocus	11 tons	87 feet
Apatosurus (Brontosaurus)	30 tons	66 feet
Brachiosaurus	85 tons	80 feet
Ornithischians		
Anatosaurus	3½ tons	33 feet
Stegosaurus	2 tons	20 feet
Triceratops	9 tons	24 feet
Panoplosaurus	4 tons	?

Mussasaurus

Compsognathus

50 ft.

10 ft.

5 ft.

0

DINOSAUR DIVERSITY

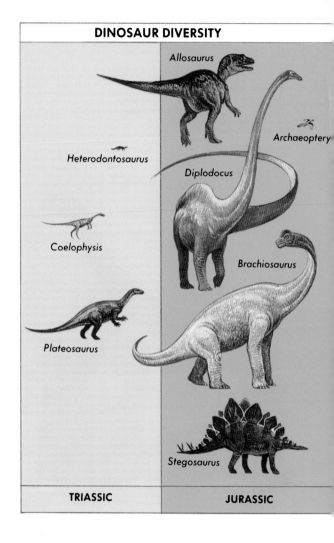

Allosaurus

Archaeopteryx

Heterodontosaurus

Diplodocus

Coelophysis

Brachiosaurus

Plateosaurus

Stegosaurus

TRIASSIC

JURASSIC

Deinonychus

Triceratops

Euoplocephalus

Protoceratops

Pachycephalosaurus

Iguanodon

Parasaurolophus

Tyrannosaurus

Styracosaurus

Ornithomimus

human for scale

CRETACEOUS

29

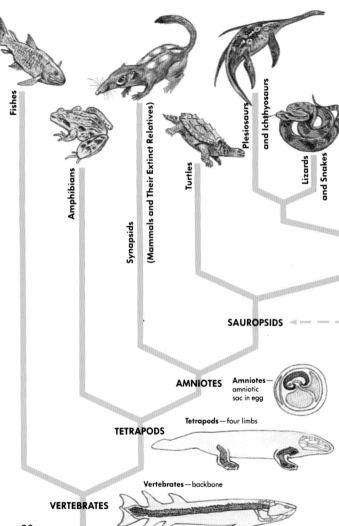

Fishes

Amphibians

Synapsids
(Mammals and Their Extinct Relatives)

Turtles

Plesiosaurs
and Ichthyosaurs

Lizards
and Snakes

SAUROPSIDS

AMNIOTES   Amniotes—
amniotic
sac in egg

Tetrapods—four limbs

TETRAPODS

Vertebrates—backbone

VERTEBRATES

30

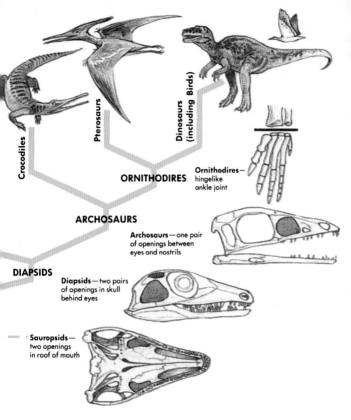

Crocodiles

Pterosaurs

Dinosaurs (including Birds)

ORNITHODIRES

Ornithodires— hingelike ankle joint

ARCHOSAURS

Archosaurs—one pair of openings between eyes and nostrils

DIAPSIDS

Diapsids—two pairs of openings in skull behind eyes

Sauropsids— two openings in roof of mouth

EVOLUTION OF ANIMALS WITH BACKBONES

Living things evolve by ancestors giving rise to descendants, similar to parents giving rise to children. A descendant organism that differs from its ancestor may give rise to new kinds of organisms. The fossil record does not document all the ancestors and their descendants, and so it is necessary to rely on characteristics of organisms to determine their relationships and evolutionary history. Derived characters inherited from a common ancestor are used to test and decide which organisms are most closely related. The key characteristics illustrated here are discussed on pp. 32-33.

KEY CHARACTERISTICS OF BACKBONED ANIMALS

Because the fossil record does not document all ancestors and their descendants, it is necessary to rely on advanced or derived characters of organisms to determine their relationships and evolutionary history. Here are the key characters defining the main groups of backboned animals (as illustrated on pp. 30-31).

backbone

VERTEBRATES A backbone consisting of block-shaped bones articulating in a long column is the character that defines this group. The backbone provides a foundation for the muscles that move the trunk and limbs. This large group includes everything on the chart, fishes to birds, as well as mammals and humans.

four limbs

TETRAPODS All the vertebrates that have four limbs with bony wrists, ankles, fingers, and toes belong in this group. Tetrapod means "four footed." In contrast to fishes, tetrapods have a greatly improved ability to move on dry land. This group consists of everything to the right of fishes on the chart—amphibians, synapsids (mammals and their extinct relatives), turtles, plesiosaurs and ichthyosaurs, lizards and snakes (which are lizards that have lost their limbs), crocodiles, pterosaurs, and dinosaurs (including birds).

amniotic sac in egg

AMNIOTES Early in the history of land vertebrates, one group evolved an egg with terrestrial adaptations—a hard shell and a series of membranes that prevent water loss and also enclose the growing embryo, thus protecting it. One of these membranes is the amnion, and so the egg is called the amniotic egg. All the animals producing amniotic eggs are called amniotes.

Amniotes are divided into two large groups. One

is the synapsids, which consists of mammals and their extinct relatives. The other is the sauropsids (below).

SAUROPSIDS One of the characteristic features of sauropsids is a pair of holes in the roof of the mouth, or palate. The function of these suborbital holes is not clearly understood. Sauropsids include turtles, lizards and snakes, crocodiles, and dinosaurs (including birds). In common terms, sauropsids are the "living reptiles," plus birds. (The word "reptile" is now generally ignored for scientific purposes because not all descendants from a common ancestor are included in the term "reptile.")

two openings in roof of mouth

DIAPSIDS Primitive sauropsids, such as turtles and their extinct relatives, have a solid skull similar to the amphibians. More advanced sauropsids have two pairs of openings behind the eyes. This group is the diapsids, the word literally meaning "two openings." These openings allow for more complex jaw muscle attachment.

two pairs of openings behind eyes

ARCHOSAURS This group has even more openings in the skull. There is a pair of openings in the snout, between the nostrils and the eyes, and another opening at the side of each lower jaw. Crocodiles, pterosaurs, and dinosaurs (including birds) are archosaurs. (See pp. 34–35.)

one pair of openings between eyes and nostrils

ORNITHODIRES Among the characters ornithodires have in common is a particular type of ankle joint. This feature—shared by pterosaurs, dinosaurs, and birds—seems to be related to a more active type of locomotion. (See pp. 36–37.)

hingelike ankle joint

EVOLUTION OF THE RULING REPTILES:
THE ARCHOSAURS

Dinosaurs and birds belong with pterosaurs and crocodiles in the group called archosaurs. Archosaur means "ruling reptile" and refers to the period of time when dinosaurs and their relatives were the prominent form of life on land.

The skull of archosaurs differs from the skull of other diapsids (p. 33) in having even more openings. There is a pair of openings in the snout between the nostrils and eyes.

Primitive
Archosaur

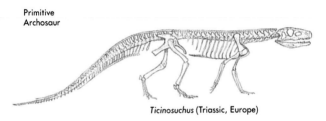

Ticinosuchus (Triassic, Europe)

Lagosuchus is the closest known relative of dinosaurs. It had a hole in the pelvic articulation—but not as large as in dinosaurs. An advanced archosaur, *Lagosuchus* had a more erect posture than the more primitive archosaurs, like *Ticinosuchus*, because the hind legs were swung toward the body to a greater extent (see pp. 36-37).

Advanced Archosaur,
close to the ancestor of dinosaurs

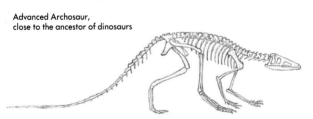

Lagosuchus (Triassic, South America)

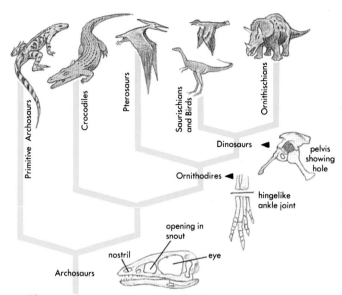

Primitive Archosaurs · Crocodiles · Pterosaurs · Saurischians and Birds · Ornithischians

Dinosaurs

pelvis showing hole

Ornithodires

hingelike ankle joint

opening in snout

nostril · eye

Archosaurs

There is also an opening on each side of the lower jaw. The function of these openings is not clear, but may have lightened the skull. The teeth are deeply rooted in bony sockets in the jaws. This type of tooth attachment is called thecodont, and is a characteristic of archosaurs.

Pterosaurs, dinosaurs, and birds are more closely related to one another than they are to other archosaurs, and belong to the group called ornithodires. The ornithodires have characters in common that seem to be related to a more active type of locomotion. Among other features, they share a particular type of ankle joint. The main joint is between the upper and lower ankle bones, and acts like a hinge, allowing only fore-and-aft movement. This type of ankle joint is consistent with a more erect stance (see p. 36) and the fore-and-aft movement of the archosaur hind limbs, and indicates animals better adapted for sustained running.

35

CHARACTERISTICS OF DINOSAURS

The popular notion of dinosaurs is not too different from Owen's—namely, huge, extinct "reptiles." But we now have a more precise—though complicated—vision of this enigmatic group. As we have seen (pp. 30-35), dinosaurs are vertebrates because they have a backbone, they are tetrapods because they have four limbs, they are amniotes because they have an amniotic membrane in their eggs, they are sauropsids because they have a pair of holes in the palate, they are diapsids because they have two openings behind the eye, they are archosaurs because they have openings in the snout, and they are ornithodires because they have a hingelike ankle joint. These characters link dinosaurs with smaller and smaller groups until finally we reach dinosaurs themselves.

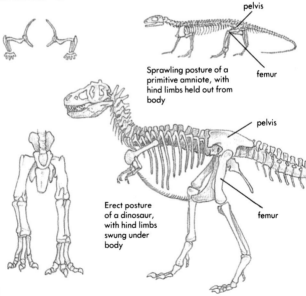

Sprawling posture of a primitive amniote, with hind limbs held out from body

pelvis

femur

Erect posture of a dinosaur, with hind limbs swung under body

pelvis

femur

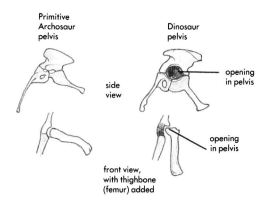

Primitive
Archosaur
pelvis

Dinosaur
pelvis

opening
in pelvis

side
view

opening
in pelvis

front view,
with thighbone
(femur) added

Dinosaurs are defined by derived characters that seem related to locomotion. The pelvis or hip bone of dinosaurs is completely vertical, and the hip socket, or acetabulum, bears the weight of the articulation of the leg at the top of the hip socket rather than on its inside as in most other tetrapods. The upper margin of the hip socket is enlarged into a shelf to support the thigh bone, or femur. The central part of the hip socket is no longer filled with bone because it no longer bears any weight. Thus a hip socket with a hole in the center and an enlarged bony rim along the upper margin is an advanced feature found only in dinosaurs and birds.

In dinosaurs and birds, these features of the hind limb-pelvis articulation mean that the hind limb is swung under the body. These animals have an upright erect posture, similar to today's running mammals. The top of the thighbone, or femur, is bent inward at an angle to fit into the pelvis so that the hind limb moves in a fore-and-aft plane.

All of the features of the limb and pelvis in dinosaurs and birds seem to be related to relatively rapid locomotion.

DINOSAUR TRACKS

When a dinosaur walked over soft mud, it sometimes left its footprints. If more mud or sand was deposited over the tracks, they occasionally became fossilized, showing us something about the living animal: whether the tail was dragged or held upright, and whether the animal was four-footed (quadrupedal) or walked on its hind legs (bipedal).

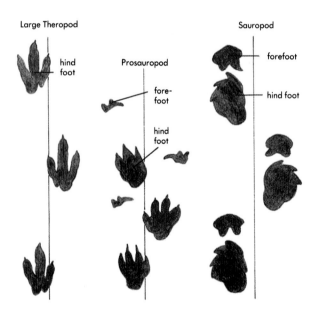

Large Theropod

hind foot

Prosauropod

fore-foot

hind foot

Sauropod

forefoot

hind foot

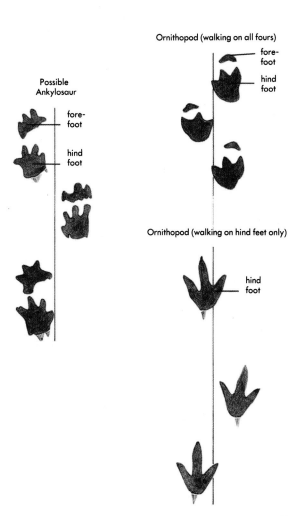

Possible
Ankylosaur

fore-
foot

hind
foot

Ornithopod (walking on all fours)

fore-
foot

hind
foot

Ornithopod (walking on hind feet only)

hind
foot

41

THE TWO MAJOR GROUPS OF DINOSAURS: SAURISCHIANS AND ORNITHISCHIANS

The classification system for dinosaurs produced in 1887 by H. G. Seeley has withstood a century of critical tests. Based on the different shapes of the three bones that fit together to form the hip, or pelvis, he divided dinosaurs into two main groups: saurischian ("reptile-hipped") dinosaurs and ornithischian ("bird-hipped") dinosaurs. "Bird-hipped" dinosaurs have similarities to birds but are not related to them. It is the "reptile-hipped" dinosaurs that are now thought to include birds.

Saurischians (pp. 46-93)

The pelvis of saurischian dinosaurs is similar to the pelvis of other primitive animals with backbones, so it is not unique for saurischians. But other characteristics of saurischians are unique to this group and show that they all had the same common ancestor.

Most obvious is the long, flexible neck, tending toward an "S" shape. This type of neck is characteristic of all the more primitive saurischians. It is secondarily shortened in some advanced groups, such as the carnosaurs (*Tyrannosaurus* and its near relatives).

The relatively large saurischian forefoot (see p. 45) has its second finger longest and the thumb strongly offset by a series of unique bone articulations. The offset thumb and other features suggest that at least some saurischians may have had greater flexibility of the forelimb, and some may have had an opposable thumb and grasping forefoot. This forefoot type is highly modified in later saurischians such as sauropods and carnosaurs.

Facing page: The two major groups of dinosaurs differ in the structure of their hips. Note the different shapes of the three bones that make up the pelvis.

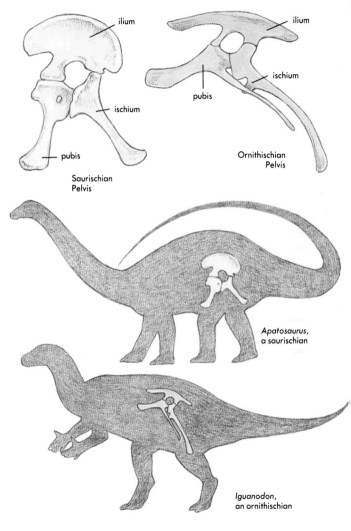

ilium

ischium

pubis

Saurischian
Pelvis

ilium

ischium

pubis

Ornithischian
Pelvis

Apatosaurus,
a saurischian

Iguanodon,
an ornithischian

43

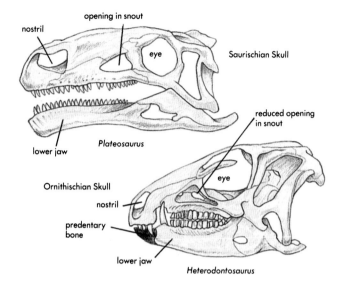

opening in snout

nostril

eye

Saurischian Skull

lower jaw

Plateosaurus

Ornithischian Skull

reduced opening in snout

eye

nostril

predentary bone

lower jaw

Heterodontosaurus

Above: A unique feature of the ornithischian skull is a beaklike bone (the predentary) in front of the teeth in the lower jaw, absent in saurischians.

Facing page: The saurischian forefoot has a strongly offset thumb (1) and a longest second finger (2), with remaining digits smaller in series. The ornithischian forefoot is more similar to the primitive archosaur condition. Later members of both groups evolved very specialized forefeet from these patterns.

Below: Saurischians have large, sharp teeth. Ornithischian teeth are usually smaller and blunter.

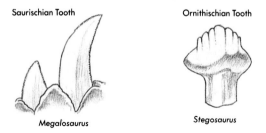

Saurischian Tooth

Ornithischian Tooth

Megalosaurus

Stegosaurus

Ornithischians (pp. 94-145)

The ornithischian pelvis has a unique feature. The bone (pubis) at the front of the pelvis has a process, or extension, that points down and backward (see p. 43). In many ornithischians, the front part of the pubis is small or absent.

The ornithischian skull has several features unique to this group. The front teeth in most ornithischians are either small or completely absent, replaced by a horny beak. An extra lower jaw bone, called the predentary, unique to the ornithischians, bears this beak.

In advanced ornithischians the teeth are complex and varied, but in the primitive types they are leaf-shaped and triangular, with a series of bumps or cusps along their edges. This leaf-shaped tooth is another unique ornithischian character. In the skull, the openings between the nostrils and eyes, characteristic of all other archosaurs, are reduced or absent. The reason is unknown.

Saurischian Forefoot

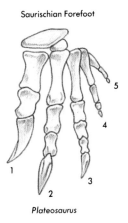

Plateosaurus

Ornithischian Forefoot

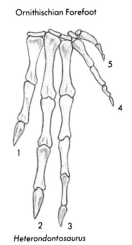

Heterondontosaurus

BRONTOSAURS AND THEIR EARLY RELATIVES

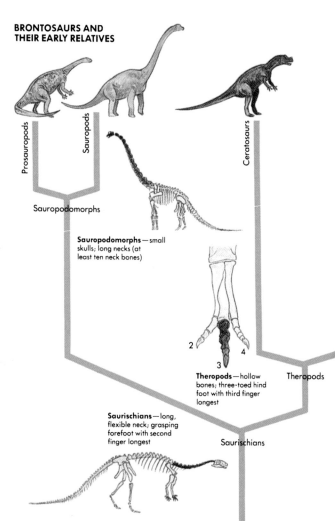

Prosauropods

Sauropods

Ceratosaurs

Sauropodomorphs

Sauropodomorphs—small skulls; long necks (at least ten neck bones)

2 3 4

Theropods—hollow bones; three-toed hind foot with third finger longest

Theropods

Saurischians—long, flexible neck; grasping forefoot with second finger longest

Saurischians

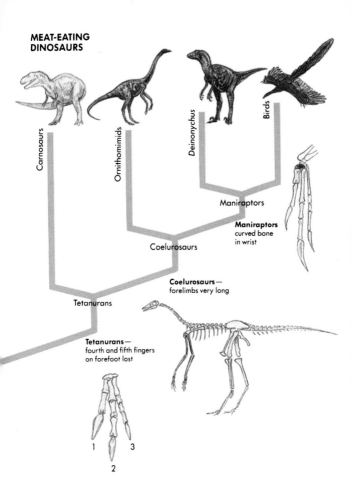

MEAT-EATING DINOSAURS

Carnosaurs

Ornithomimids

Deinonychus

Birds

Maniraptors

Maniraptors
curved bone in wrist

Coelurosaurs

Coelurosaurs—
forelimbs very long

Tetanurans

Tetanurans—
fourth and fifth fingers on forefoot lost

1 3
2

EVOLUTION OF SAURISCHIAN DINOSAURS

47

GIANT DINOSAURS AND THEIR KIN

Gigantic dinosaurs of the "brontosaur" type are called sauropods. A diverse group known from the Jurassic and Cretaceous, sauropods were preceded by a Triassic group called the prosauropods, or "before sauropods." Together these groups are known as the sauropodomorphs.

Sauropodomorphs have long necks, long tails, and relatively small skulls. The necks have ten or more vertebrae, and the pencil-shaped teeth have serrations along the top. In some advanced sauropods, these serrations are lost. The thumb or first finger on the forefoot is stout and large, with an unusually large claw. The other fingers are relatively small. In the more advanced sauropods, such as *Diplodocus* and *Brachiosaurus*, many of the fingers are greatly reduced, formed into a heavy, columnar foot. The large claw on the thumb persists, however, and sticks out.

In prosauropods, the hind foot resembles the primitive

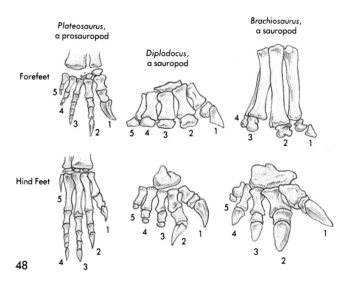

Plateosaurus,
a prosauropod

Diplodocus,
a sauropod

Brachiosaurus,
a sauropod

Forefeet

Hind Feet

dinosaur condition, in that the second, third, and fourth fingers are nearly equal in length and longer than the other two, and the fifth finger is reduced to a small bone. In sauropods, the fingers are reduced and shortened, but in some the claws are retained. The hind foot has a large "heel" of soft tissue and relatively little flexibility.

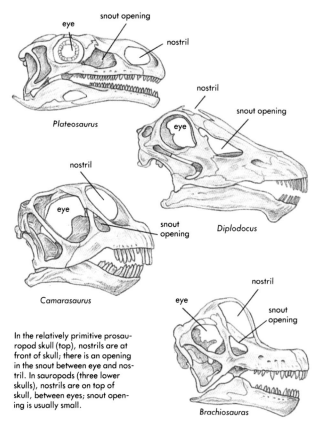

eye
snout opening
nostril

Plateosaurus

nostril
snout opening
eye

Diplodocus

nostril
eye
snout opening

Camarasaurus

nostril
eye
snout opening

Brachiosauras

In the relatively primitive prosauropod skull (top), nostrils are at front of skull; there is an opening in the snout between eye and nostril. In sauropods (three lower skulls), nostrils are on top of skull, between eyes; snout opening is usually small.

49

▶ PLATEOSAURUS

Age: Late Triassic; some near relatives from Early Jurassic. **Fossils found:** Europe; near relatives on all continents except Antarctica. **Size:** 26 feet long. **Features:** a prosauropod; large claw on thumb; long neck with small skull; apparently both bipedal and quadrupedal.

The prosauropods are not a diverse group and are all similar to *Plateosaurus*. They had narrow, sharp-pointed teeth with serrated margins. They are presumed to have been vegetarians, using their teeth to slice rather than to mash, but there have been suggestions that they were either meat eaters or omnivores—eating a wide variety of plant and animal food.

Plateosaurus had larger hind limbs than front limbs, but it is not known whether it ran on its hind legs, walked on all fours, or perhaps did both. Trackways (p. 40) seem to show that prosauropods were mainly quadrupedal. The large claw on the thumb could have been used both for defense and for obtaining food. Prosauropods extended from the Middle Triassic to the Early Jurassic, but Middle Triassic ones are

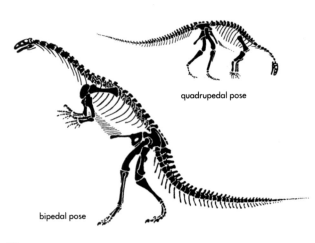

quadrupedal pose

bipedal pose

poorly known. They were probably the first large plant eaters among the dinosaurs and are known from large numbers of individuals on many continents. A quarry in southern Germany yielded the remains of about 40 individuals, though few of the skeletons were articulated. Others have been found in northeastern and southwestern United States, South Africa, South America, and China.

▶ MUSSASAURUS

Age: Late Triassic. **Fossils found:** Argentina. **Size:** known specimens 8 inches long; adults presumably larger. **Features:** a prosauropod; smallest known dinosaur.

Mussasaurus is known from very young individuals. Large eyes and brain and thin, fragile bones indicate they are juveniles. Structure of pelvis and limbs suggests prosauropods, but absence of adult specimens prevents comparisons with others.

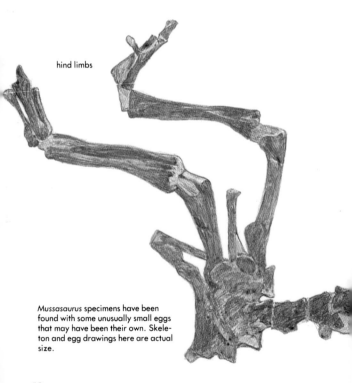

hind limbs

Mussasaurus specimens have been found with some unusually small eggs that may have been their own. Skeleton and egg drawings here are actual size.

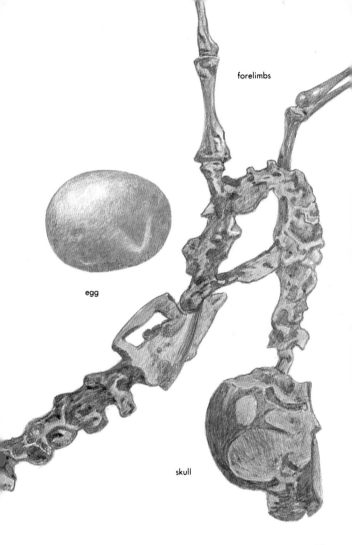

forelimbs

egg

skull

53

■ DIPLODOCUS

Age: Late Jurassic. **Fossils found:** western United States. **Size:** 87 feet long. **Features:** a sauropod; one of the longest dinosaurs, but slim-bodied with relatively light limbs; nostrils high on skull between eyes; tail very long and thin.

Diplodocus is one of the sauropods, perhaps the most spectacular group of dinosaurs because of their great size. *Diplodocus* had an extremely long neck, with 15 neck bones; the even longer tail had 70 bones, the last ones being fairly small rods. Its front limbs were distinctly shorter than its hind limbs. In contrast to the thick-limbed *Camarasaurus* and *Brachiosaurus*, *Diplodocus* had thin leg bones for a sauropod. While *Brachiosaurus* and its even more gigantic relative *Ultrasaurus* are speculated to have weighed in excess of 80 tons, *Diplodocus* was probably about 10 to 12 tons—even though it was one of the longest sauropods.

Diplodocus is one of the titanosaurs, a group of similar-appearing sauropods that all had long, narrow skulls with the nostril openings high on the skull between the eyes. The teeth of titanosaurs were simple, long pegs situated at the front of the mouth. Titanosaurs have been found throughout the world.

Diplodocus was first discovered in 1877 near Canyon City, Colorado, by S.W. Williston, and later named by O.C. Marsh. The original specimen consisted of only a few bones, but better skeletons became available in 1899.

APATOSAURUS

Age: Late Jurassic. **Fossils found:** western United States. **Size:** 70 feet long, 14 feet at shoulder. **Features:** a sauropod; similar to *Diplodocus*, but with a stockier neck and body.

Apatosaurus is the correct name for the dinosaur commonly known as "*Brontosaurus*." The first fossils of this animal were incomplete, and different bones were given different names because it was not realized that they belonged to the same species. Later, when better specimens were discovered, *Apatosaurus* was determined to be the correct name because it was used first, even though "*Brontosaurus*" had been used in many popular books.

In 1873, when O.C. Marsh first reconstructed the dinosaur we now know as *Apatosaurus*, he did not have a skeleton with a skull. Doing the best he could, he used the skull of *Camarasaurus*. In 1915, W.J. Holland was collecting dinosaurs for the Carnegie Museum when he found two *Apatosaurus* specimens. Very close, but not actually articulated, was a skull that looked like *Diplodocus*. Holland felt this skull belonged to *Apatosaurus*, but he was not sure because *Apatosaurus* was thought to be related to *Camarasaurus*.

In the late 1970s, sauropod expert John McIntosh recognized from field reports that Holland was right. *Apatosaurus* is quite closely related to *Diplodocus*, not *Camarasaurus*, and therefore probably had a similar skull. Because of the very limited nature of fossils, it is easy to be wrong in paleontology!

Apatosaurus and *Diplodocus* are closely related and have long skulls with the nostrils high up between the eyes. *Camarasaurus* has a shorter skull with nostrils in front of the eyes.

nostril

eye

Apatosaurus

nostril

eye

Camarasaurus

■ BRACHIOSAURUS

Age: Late Jurassic. **Fossils found:** western United States and Tanzania. **Size:** 75 feet long. **Features:** huge sauropod; giraffelike posture, with hind legs shorter than front legs; massive body; relatively short tail; long neck with very large neckbones; skull short, with large nostrils separated by thin bar of bone.

Brachiosaurus is both the largest dinosaur known from a good skeleton and the largest mounted dinosaur. The animal's estimated weight has been guessed at more than 80 tons. Its legs, like those of its near relatives, were immense columns, apparently capable of supporting the animal on dry land.

The small size of the skull and the simple teeth have made it difficult to speculate on these dinosaurs' diet. They were apparently plant eaters, but no stomach contents or other clues are available. The neck vertebrae of *Brachiosaurus* were more than 3 feet long, with large, muscle-scarred spines. Large cavities penetrating the bones produced a complex series of air spaces that greatly lightened the neck.

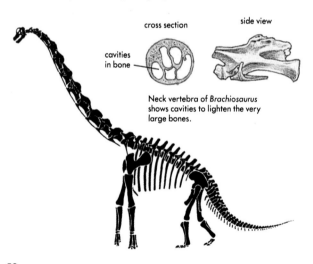

cross section

side view

cavities in bone

Neck vertebra of *Brachiosaurus* shows cavities to lighten the very large bones.

Although early dinosaur workers around the turn of the century had concluded that the skeleton should be mounted in a sprawling position, sauropod trackways (pp. 40-41 and 62-63) show a relatively narrow gait, indicating an upright, elephantlike stance. As these trackways do not seem to have tail drags, sauropods are usually shown with the tail held horizontally off the ground.

■ CAMARASAURUS

Age: Late Jurassic. **Fossils found:** western United States. **Size:** up to 60 feet long. **Features:** medium-size sauropod, generally bulkier and with shorter neck than other sauropods; skull relatively large and short, with large nostrils separated by thin bar of bone.

Camarasaurus is one of the best-known sauropods. A skeleton of an immature *Camarasaurus*, 17 feet long and about one-fourth the size of a full-grown adult, is the most complete sauropod skeleton known.

The way of life of sauropods has been the subject of much speculation. Early workers were so impressed by their huge size and great weight that they thought sauropods could not walk on dry land because the cartilage and bone in their joints would be crushed. Therefore, sauropods were pictured as semiaquatic swamp and river dwellers. The nostrils, placed high on the head, have been suggested as a device for "snorkeling," an aquatic adaptation that allowed only the tip of the head to come up for air. This would have been unlikely, however, due to the pressure of water on the chest.

Sauropod trackways show that at least some sauropods walked on all fours without support from floating. But other trackways show swimming sauropods using only the forefeet for "poling" along the bottom. Recent speculations, interpreting dinosaurs using a more mammalian model, depict sauropods as upland dwellers, galloping in herds and browsing on high trees.

What is correct? There were many species of sauropods; they lived for more than 100 million years and probably occupied many different habitats. It may be too simple to ascribe one pattern to all of them. We will probably never know the real range of habitats for this group.

Facing page: Trackways show some sauropods were quadrupedal, walking on all fours (top); others show swimming sauropods using their forefeet to "pole" along the bottom (middle). Some sauropods may have been "tripedal," using the tail for support (bottom).

SAUROPOD TRACKWAYS

Trackways are formed when animals walk over moist mud or sand and leave imprints. They are useful records of actual activities of prehistoric animals at specific times and places.

Identifying which genus made a particular trackway is virtually impossible, but the general group of dinosaurs that formed it can be determined. For instance, the tracks of sauropods are unique—their front legs produced horseshoe-shaped prints with a single large claw on the thumb; the hind legs left large oval prints showing claws and a thick, fibrous "heel."

The most famous sauropod trackways are a series of sites in the Early Cretaceous Glen Rose Formation of Texas. The Mayan Ranch trackway shows only the front legs and one hind leg imprint where the trackway changes directions.

hind foot mark

Mayan Ranch trackway, Cretaceous of Texas

These are believed to show a sauropod swimming, pushing along its front feet and using a kick from the hind foot to change direction.

Also at Glen Rose is a set of 23 overlapping trackways made by 23 sauropods of different sizes walking in about the same direction. These were probably formed along the margin of a body of water rather than by an organized herd, as often speculated.

For years sauropods were illustrated with the tail on the ground. As sauropods had no accessory articulations or special modifications of the tail bones to hold them stiff, this depiction was logical. However, the absence of tail drags in any of the sauropod trackways indicates that the tail was held erect, a position that is now shown in sauropod reconstructions.

SAUROPOD BURIAL SITES

Sauropods and other Late Jurassic dinosaurs have been found in a series of bone beds in western United States. The museum at Dinosaur National Monument near Vernal, Utah, was built on an exposure of such a bone bed, one with over 2,000 bones of both adults and juveniles still in place.

The rocks containing the bones had been sandbars in a large river system similar to the present-day Mississippi Delta. The silt-laden, sluggish river meandered through low-

Although the lowland, meandering river system seems to have been a region where dinosaur fossils were commonly formed, other environments have also

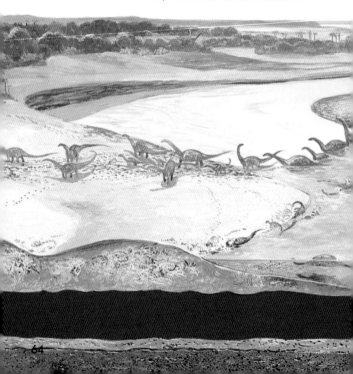

lands covered with conifers and other gymnosperms. Dinosaurs that died in or near the river would have been carried to places where silt and sand were accumulating rapidly, or washed onto sandbars during floods. Skeletons buried quickly remained articulated, but most were separated.

Although the lowland, meandering river system seems to have been a region where dinosaur fossils were commonly formed, other environments have also yielded dinosaurs. Upland swamps, lakes, streams, windblown dunes, and even the edges of seas have yielded dinosaur fossils.

yielded dinosaurs. Upland swamps, lakes, streams, windblown dunes, and even the edges of seas have yielded dinosaur fossils.

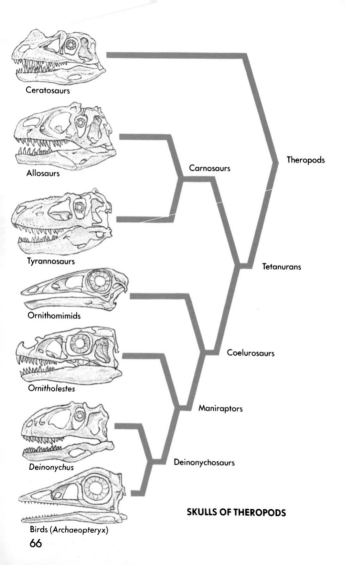

Ceratosaurs

Allosaurs

Carnosaurs

Tyrannosaurs

Theropods

Tetanurans

Ornithomimids

Coelurosaurs

Ornitholestes

Maniraptors

Deinonychus

Deinonychosaurs

Birds (Archaeopteryx)

SKULLS OF THEROPODS

MEAT-EATING DINOSAURS: THEROPODS AND BIRDS

Theropod, meaning Beast Foot, is a group including *Tyrannosaurus*, the most immense meat-eating animal that has ever existed, and hummingbirds, among the smallest of all amniotes. That birds are living theropods shows the great diversity of this group. Known from the Late Triassic, hence among the earliest of the dinosaurs, large theropods persisted until the end of the Cretaceous.

Theropods include a great variety of extinct meat-eating creatures. Carnosaurs, such as *Allosaurus* and *Tyrannosaurus*, had large skulls with stout teeth that could have penetrated the thick skin of other dinosaurs. Smaller theropods, like *Ornitholestes* and *Deinonychus*, presumably pursued smaller prey. Their skulls were lightly built, with smaller, more delicate teeth.

Modern birds lack teeth and have a horny beak, but *Archaeopteryx*, the Jurassic bird, had many small teeth and no beak. Another group of theropods, the ornithomimids, also lost their teeth and replaced them with a horny beak. Their skull was lightly built and birdlike, with very large eyes and a brain that was the same relative size as in modern birds. Those with large brains presumably preyed on active, agile animals.

Skull modifications of theropods are related clearly to prey and feeding methods. Their front limbs also show modifications that are in some cases extreme. In tyrannosaurs, the already very small forefoot was reduced to only two fingers, but other theropods had large front legs that were probably used to seize and manipulate prey. The peculiar changes in the forelimbs of maniraptors ("hand catchers") included modifications that in birds were for flying.

▶ COELOPHYSIS

Age: Late Triassic. **Fossils found:** western United States; near relatives on all other continents except Antarctica. **Size:** about 6 feet long. **Features:** small, bipedal theropod with long, narrow skull and relatively elongate forelimbs.

One of the most exciting events in the annals of 20th century dinosaur lore was Edwin H. Colbert's discovery of more than 20 *Coelophysis* skeletons in a mass burial at Ghost Ranch in New Mexico. This remains the best sample of a Triassic theropod, a group otherwise known only from poorly preserved specimens.

Coelophysis appears to have been an agile carnivore, with a long skull and plenty of sharp teeth. Specializations of the

ankle joint and pelvis suggest it is most closely related to *Ceratosaurus* and *Dilophosaurus,* both larger meat-eating dinosaurs.

Another interesting feature of the Ghost Ranch find was the presence of young dinosaur bones inside the stomachs of some of the specimens. These bones probably represent cannibalistic meals.

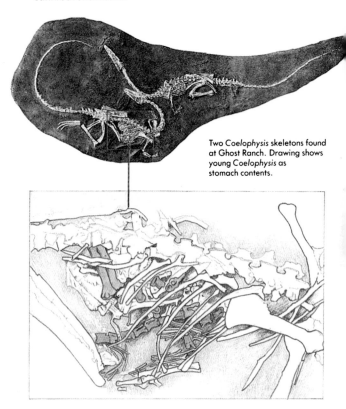

Two *Coelophysis* skeletons found at Ghost Ranch. Drawing shows young *Coelophysis* as stomach contents.

■DILOPHOSAURUS

Age: Early Jurassic. **Fossils found:** Arizona. **Size:** 20 feet long. **Features:** medium-sized theropod with a pair of thin crests extending along the skull above the eyes.

Dilophosaurus had thin-walled crests on its skull, beginning near the nose and extending back above the eyes. The function of these crests is unknown. The remainder of the skull had single rows of sharp, curved teeth and relatively large openings.

Fossils of *Dilophosaurus* were first found in 1942 on the Navajo Indian Reservation in northern Arizona. It is one of the few relatively complete dinosaurs known from the Early Jurassic. The deposits containing *Dilophosaurus* are a series of sands and clays called the Kayenta Formation, formed by streams and ponds. They contain an incredible sample of vertebrate life from the little-known Early Jurassic, including turtles, flying reptiles, amphibians, crocodiles, mammallike reptiles, and some of the oldest mammals.

skull of *Dilophosaurus*

crest

eye

nostril

restoration of head of *Dilophosaurus*

73

■ CERATOSAURUS

Age: Late Jurassic. **Fossils found:** North America; near relatives in Africa.
Size: 20 feet long. **Features:** theropod similar to but half as large as
Allosaurus, with a nose horn and four fingers on forelimbs.

As in the other carnosaurs, *Ceratosaurus* had a large head
with a short, thick neck, relatively short forelimbs, large,
powerful hind legs, and well-developed curved claws on both
forefeet and hind feet. The weight of the skull was reduced
by large openings, and the long, curved teeth were well
rooted in the skull and jaw. Older teeth were continually
being replaced by new ones during its lifespan (p. 68). At
any one time, the mouth contained a mixture of large, old
teeth and smaller, new ones.

The "horn" above the nose, giving *Ceratosaurus* its name, was actually a thin crest that did not necessarily bear a horny covering. *Ceratosaurus* had low brow ridges above the eyes. In *Allosaurus* the ridges were larger and roughened. *Dilophosaurus* had a pair of long, thin crests on top of the skull, and *Tyrannosaurus* had roughened brow ridges. The purposes of these various ridges is completely unknown, but they are found in many theropods.

The ceratosaurs—*Ceratosaurus, Coelophysis,* and *Dilophosaurus*—are more primitive than other theropods because, among other features, they had four fingers on each forelimb. The fourth finger was very small. The tetanurans—which are all the theropods *except* ceratosaurs—lost the fourth finger, and the second finger was largest.

As with so many facets of dinosaur life, the behavior of predatory dinosaurs has been the subject of much speculation. Ideas have been advanced that theropods hunted in packs in order to bring down large dinosaurs such as sauropods. Some have suggested that very large theropods were too slow to catch live prey because of their size and had to be scavengers. The evidence available from skeletons, trackways, and burial environments is inadequate to seriously test these ideas.

■ ALLOSAURUS

Age: Late Jurassic. **Fossils found:** western North America. **Size:** 30 to 40 feet long. **Features:** theropod with three well-developed fingers and claws on each hand; skull relatively large, with low brow horns.

Allosaurus, best known of the Jurassic carnosaurs, was a large, bipedal animal with small but functional forelimbs. Each of the three fingers had large claws, those on the thumb and forefinger largest. The skull was lightened by many openings. In most dinosaurs, the openings between the nose and eyes were small, but in *Allosaurus* and other carnivorous dinosaurs, they were the largest openings in the skull. The large, curved teeth had serrated edges, as in other meat eaters, and extended from the front of the mouth to the back.

Allosaurus was named by O.C. Marsh in the 1880s, but was not described in detail until the work of C.W. Gilmore

Restoration painting of *Allosaurus* by Charles R. Knight, based on the skeleton shown at top of the facing page.

possible tooth marks

Top: *Allosaurus* skeleton in the American Museum of Natural History, mounted over a partial *Apatosaurus* skeleton. Bottom: Tail bones from the *Apatosaurus* skeleton above, showing grooves that may have been made by *Allosaurus* teeth.

of the Smithsonian Institution in the 1920s. A spectacular deposit of *Allosaurus* bones, the Cleveland-Lloyd Quarry, was discovered in 1927 in Utah. Disarticulated remains of at least 44 individuals of *Allosaurus* were collected from this quarry. They range in size from presumed juveniles about 10 feet long to adults about 40 feet long.

Allosaurus was the subject of a Charles R. Knight painting based on a skeleton from the Cope Collection mounted in the American Museum of Natural History at the turn of the century. This skeleton is mounted over a partial skeleton of *Apatosaurus*. The tail bones of the *Apatosaurus* skeleton have grooves in them—damage that may have been inflicted by a carnivorous dinosaur.

ALBERTOSAURUS

Age: Late Cretaceous. **Fossils found:** western North America. **Size:** 26 feet long. **Features:** a theropod; similar to *Tyrannosaurus* in having a very large skull and only two fingers on each of the very small forelimbs; differs in being about half the size of *Tyrannosaurus*.

In the last part of the Age of Dinosaurs, the Jurassic theropods such as *Allosaurus* and *Ceratosaurus* were replaced by Cretaceous carnosaurs such as *Albertosaurus*, *Tarbosaurus*, and *Tyrannosaurus*. These predators differed from the earlier meat eaters in having somewhat different body proportions. (See *Tyrannosaurus* on p. 80.) They had relatively larger heads and hind limbs, and much smaller forelimbs. Their skulls were huge biting mechanisms with very deep bone areas for the attachment of large teeth. The lower jaws were deep, and had enlarged areas for muscle attachment. These animals were presumably capable of killing and eating almost any of their equally large contemporaries.

The very small size of the forelimbs and the reduction of fingers to only two suggest that the forelimbs had only limited use. Perhaps they were not used for much of anything.

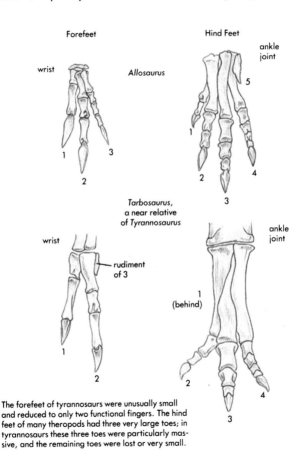

Forefeet

Hind Feet

ankle joint

wrist

Allosaurus

1

3

2

5

1

2

4

3

Tarbosaurus,
a near relative
of *Tyrannosaurus*

ankle joint

wrist

rudiment
of 3

1

2

1
(behind)

2

4

3

The forefeet of tyrannosaurs were unusually small and reduced to only two functional fingers. The hind feet of many theropods had three very large toes; in tyrannosaurs these three toes were particularly massive, and the remaining toes were lost or very small.

TYRANNOSAURUS

Age: Late Cretaceous. **Fossils found:** North America; near relatives in Asia. **Size:** 40 feet long. **Features:** theropod with very large head and hind legs, very small forelimbs with only two fingers; deep jaws with large, curved teeth.

Tyrannosaurus was a huge carnivorous dinosaur, the largest meat-eating animal known. Its discovery, in 1902, was one of the great moments in paleontology.

Tyrannosaurus

A juvenile tyrannosaur, possibly *Albertosaurus*

Barnum Brown, champion bone hunter of the American Museum of Natural History, collected skeletons of *Tyrannosaurus* in 1902 and 1908 in the Hell Creek region of Montana. The specimens were found in sandstones formed in a vast river system and later cemented by very hard minerals, which caused considerable problems during collection. Some parts of the skeleton could not be separated and had to be removed in huge blocks. The pelvis, or hip, was removed in one block that weighed more than two tons. This and the other blocks were dragged and carried by wagons pulled by teams of horses 130 miles to the nearest railway.

With the expenditure of great energy and manpower, the specimens of *Tyrannosaurus* were prepared and mounted at the American Museum of Natural History in only a few years. The best skeleton is still on display in New York. The other skeleton was sold to the Carnegie Museum in Pittsburgh, where it is on exhibit.

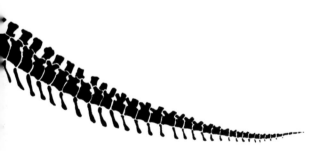

ORNITHOMIMUS

Age: Late Cretaceous. **Fossils found:** North America; close relatives in Europe, Africa, and Asia. **Size:** 10 to 14 feet long. **Features:** theropod with small skull lacking teeth but with a horny bill and very large eyes; large, curved claws on relatively long forelimbs.

Ornithomimus is often called the Ostrich Dinosaur because of its similarity to ostriches in size and appearance. This lightly built dinosaur was apparently adapted for rapid running on its hind legs. The body was held horizontally, with the long tail extending backward for balance. The neck was long and seems to have been very flexible. The skull lacked teeth and had very large openings for the eyes, which may have been the largest of any of the dinosaurs. The jaws were probably covered with a horny bill, as in birds. The brain was unusually large, having about the same proportion to body size as in modern birds. The forelimbs, which had three fingers, probably weren't used for locomotion.

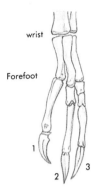

wrist

Forefoot

1

2 3

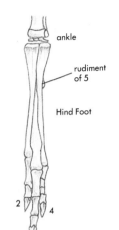

ankle

rudiment of 5

Hind Foot

2 4

3

The forelimbs of ornithomimids had three long fingers with sharp claws and may have been used for grasping prey. The hind limbs had three slender fingers and were adapted for rapid running.

COMPSOGNATHUS

Age: Late Jurassic. **Fossils found:** Europe. **Size:** 2 feet long. **Features:** a theropod; small size and only two fingers on each forelimb separate it from the other birdlike theropods.

Only about the size of a chicken, *Compsognathus* is one of the smallest adult dinosaurs known. Like *Ornitholestes*, it was lightly built, with a long neck and tail. The hind legs were used for bipedal running; the small forelimbs, with only two fingers, were apparently for catching prey.

In contrast to other dinosaurs, something definite is known about the prey of *Compsognathus*, for one specimen has been found with the remains of a meal inside its rib cage. John Ostrom of Yale University has determined that these remains belonged to *Bavarisaurus*, a small, fast-running lizard. This find demonstrates that *Compsognathus* had the agility and coordination to hunt those animals.

Compsognathus is a rare dinosaur, for only a few specimens are known. These occur in the Solnhofen Formation in Germany, a marine limestone that was formed in a warm, shallow sea interspersed with coral islands. Most of the fossils in this formation were ocean dwellers, but occasionally there are fossils of species such as *Compsognathus* and of lizards that lived on the shores. There are also fossils of pterosaurs and of *Archaeopteryx*, the oldest bird.

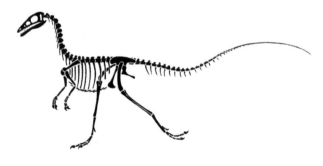

ORNITHOLESTES

Age: Late Jurassic. **Fossils found:** western North America; close relatives in Europe, Asia, Africa, and Australia. **Size:** 6½ feet long. **Features:** theropod; small skull with small, pointed teeth; forelimbs with three fingers, similar to early birds.

Ornitholestes retained many of the primitive features characterizing the birdlike group of meat-eating dinosaurs. It had hollow bones, a light skull with large openings, and forelimbs with three well-developed clawed fingers. This small dinosaur was presumably an active predator, running on its hind legs and relying on speed and agility to capture small animals.

When first discovered in the 1890s, it was named "bird robber" (*Ornitholestes*), suggesting that it was able to hunt and kill birds. There is no way to determine whether or not this was true, but it is possible. Interestingly, *Ornitholestes* is now thought to be one of the dinosaurs closely related to birds—rather than a hunter of them.

Ornitholestes was one of the prize fossils collected by the American Museum of Natural History in 1890 in the famous Bone Cabin Quarry of southern Wyoming. No better skeletons of *Ornitholestes* have ever been found.

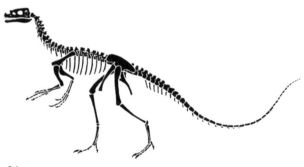

DEINONYCHUS

Age: Early Cretaceous. **Fossils found:** Montana. **Size:** 7 feet long. **Features:** theropod with very large claw on second toe of hind foot; tail stiffened by long processes on vertebrae.

Although this small theropod is superficially similar to such meat eaters as *Allosaurus*, it has important differences in the feet that show it must have had a very distinctive way of life. The normal theropod hind foot with three strong toes is modified in *Deinonychus*: only two of the toes were actually used in running or walking. The remaining toe has a disproportionately large claw, one so large, in fact, that it must have been retracted during locomotion. When bent down, the claw must have served as a formidable weapon, presumably used in attacking and killing prey.

The structure of the pelvis and hind leg also differs from other dinosaurs, and indicates the presence of particularly powerful musculature. The whole combination of features found in *Deinonychus* suggests a very active, aggressive carnivore.

The forelimbs of *Deinonychus* (p. 93) are strikingly similar to those of primitive birds and are part of the evidence that birds actually are dinosaurs.

The unusually large claw on second toe of hind foot was probably used in catching or attacking prey. The claw was apparently rotated upward during locomotion.

■ ARCHAEOPTERYX

Age: Late Jurassic. **Fossils found:** Europe. **Size:** 2 to 3 feet long. **Features:** a theropod; skeleton very much like *Ornitholestes* or *Compsognathus* but covered with feathers and having a wishbone (furcula).

Archaeopteryx is the oldest animal definitely known to be a bird. A number of specimens from the Late Jurassic Solnhofen Limestone Formation of Germany show detailed imprints of feathers.

This limestone was originally an extremely fine-grained mud, formed at the bottom of a shallow sea, and *Archaeopteryx* lived near or above this sea. Some apparently fell into the sea and sank to the bottom, where their bones were preserved and the feathers impressed into the mud.

Although *Archaeopteryx* had feathers, could it fly as well as modern birds? Probably not. Modern birds have a greatly expanded keel, or breastbone, to which large flight muscles are attached. *Archaeopteryx* did not have this breastbone and so probably did not have large flight muscles. But it could probably fly or glide to some extent.

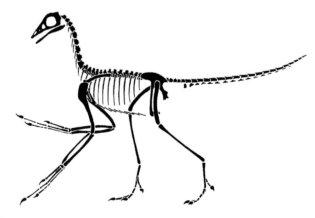

Although *Archaeopteryx* feathers themselves were not preserved, this limestone, studied under a microscope, reveals impressions that show the detailed structure of bird feathers.

BIRDS ARE DINOSAURS

The discovery and study of *Archaeopteryx* and the birdlike dinosaurs like *Ornitholestes* and *Deinonychus* give important clues about the evolution of birds. Although actual evolutionary lineages cannot be seen directly in the layers of rocks, fossils do provide information about the characters of extinct species that can be used to test evolutionary ideas. *Archaeopteryx* and dinosaurs are good examples of this use of fossils.

Dinosaurs and birds share the following unique characters:

1. ankle joint with fore-and-aft motion formed by some of the ankle bones being tightly attached to the lower leg bones (pp. 31-33)

2. upright or erect limbs (p. 36)

3. "extra" holes in the skull and jaws (pp. 31-33)

In addition, some small theropod dinosaurs, such as *Ornitholestes* and *Deinonychus,* are particularly close to birds and have the following derived characters found also in *Archaeopteryx*:

1. forelimb with three elongated fingers and a specialized wrist joint

2. hollow bones

3. pelvis with pubis swung backward

These fossils show how birds evolved from a particular group of small predatory dinosaurs. We can consider birds "living dinosaurs."

Were some dinosaurs like *Ornitholestes* "warm-blooded," with high energy rates like modern birds? Was *Archaeopteryx* more like crocodiles or like living birds in its biology? We cannot answer these questions. Fossils help us answer questions about evolution, but extinct animals give very little information about their way of life and biology.

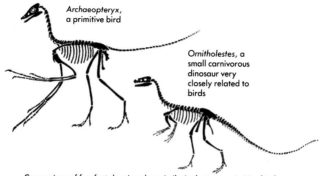

Archaeopteryx, a primitive bird

Ornitholestes, a small carnivorous dinosaur very closely related to birds

Comparison of forefeet showing close similarity between primitive birds and certain small carnivorous dinosaurs

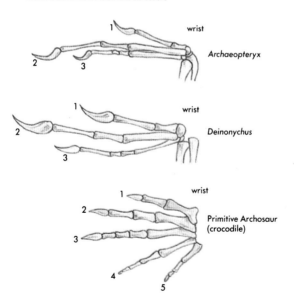

wrist

1

2

3

Archaeopteryx

wrist

1

2

3

Deinonychus

wrist

1

2

3

4

5

Primitive Archosaur (crocodile)

ARMORED DINOSAURS

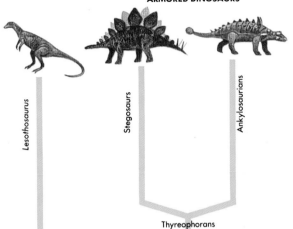

Lesothosaurus

Stegosaurs

Ankylosaurians

Thyreophorans

Thyreophorans—
bony plates and
spikes embedded in
skin

Genasaurians

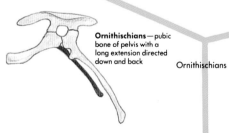

Ornithischians—pubic
bone of pelvis with a
long extension directed
down and back

Ornithischians

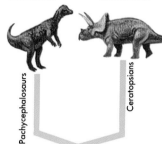

DUCKBILLS AND THEIR EARLY RELATIVES

BONE-HEADED DINOSAURS

HORNED DINOSAURS

Heterodontosaurus

Iguanodonts and Hadrosaurs

Pachycephalosaurs

Ceratopsians

Euornithopods

Marginocephalians

Marginocephalians — bony shelf extending over back of skull

Euornithopods — articulation of lower jaw and skull below level of tooth row

Cerapods

Cerapods — cheek teeth with thicker enamel on one side

Genasaurians — tooth rows recessed from edge of jaws to form cheeks; no teeth in front of skull

EVOLUTION OF ORNITHISCHIAN DINOSAURS

ORNITHISCHIAN SKULLS

The great differences in the skulls of ornithischian dinosaurs reflect the diversity of the group. A great evolutionary distance separates the primitive *Lesothosaurus* from such bizarre

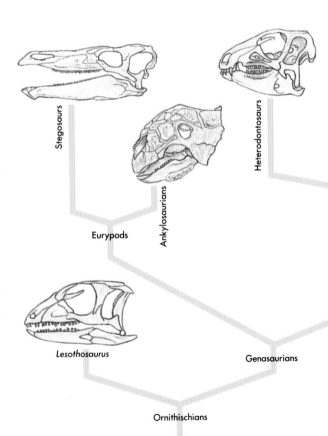

Stegosaurs

Heterodontosaurs

Ankylosaurians

Eurypods

Lesothosaurus

Genasaurians

Ornithischians

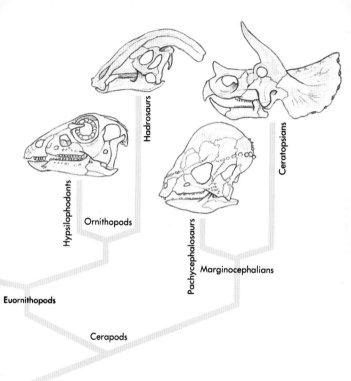

Hypsilophodonts

Hadrosaurs

Ceratopsians

Ornithopods

Pachycephalosaurs

Marginocephalians

Euornithopods

Cerapods

animals as pachycephalosaurs, ceratopsians, and hadrosaurs. And yet all bear the marks of a common ancestor.

They all have a separate toothless element, the predentary, at the front of the lower jaw, and the antorbital opening (between nostril and eye) is small or absent.

In *Lesothosaurus*, the teeth are arranged around the margin of the jaws; in genasaurians, the teeth on the sides of the jaws are recessed, forming a cheek.

FEET OF ORNITHISCHIAN DINOSAURS

While ornithischian feet do not show the extensive adaptations seen in saurischians, they do reflect adaptations for locomotion and support.

Ornithischian forelimbs show a range of variation—from the solid forefoot of *Stegosaurus*, in which most of the finger joints are lost, to the long and slender forefoot of *Heterodontosaurus*, which seems to have been quite flexible, possibly permitting some manipulation of food. The iguanodonts and hadrosaurs have forefeet with distinctly elongated bases (metacarpals), with the three middle fingers strong and solid. The claws on the middle fingers are usually expanded and hooflike. These dinosaurs may have been quadrupedal when

Forefeet

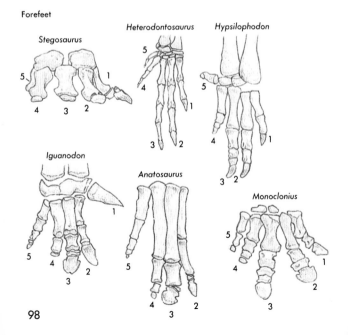

walking. The hypsilophodonts did not depart significantly from the more primitive *Heterodontosaurus* forefoot, but their fingers are heavier and less flexible, as in the more advanced ornithopods.

Ornithischian hind feet show that, in most groups, they were the major weight-bearing element. The smaller, more generalized ornithischians have lighter bones, long and slender, as in *Hypsilophodon* and *Heterodontosaurus*. The ornithopods, such as *Iguanodon* and *Anatosaurus*, are three-toed, with the first and fifth toes greatly reduced. The remaining three toes are strong and thick, capable of supporting a larger, heavy animal. *Stegosaurus* and *Monoclonius* have thick, columnar feet, *Monoclonius* retaining four functional toes.

Hindfeet

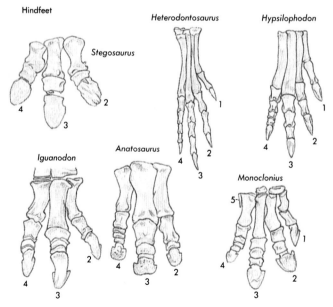

99

■ SCUTELLOSAURUS

Age: Early Jurassic. **Fossils found:** southwestern United States. **Size:** 4 feet long. **Features:** small, primitive ornithischian; probably bipedal; covered with small bony plates.

The ankylosaurs and stegosaurs are united in the group of thyreophorans (p. 94) on the basis of bony armor in the skin. *Scutellosaurus* is a primitive member of this group; it had bony armor, but lacked other distinctive features of either ankylosaurs or stegosaurs. In contrast to such late thyreophorans as stegosaurs and ankylosaurs, *Scutellosaurus* had no tail club or spikes.

Scutellosaurus was probably bipedal. But as with many dinosaurs that had small but not tiny forelimbs, it probably could have moved on all fours as well. Although not very well preserved, the specimens of *Scutellosaurus* from the Early Jurassic Kayenta Formation do provide an interesting comparison with the later stegosaurs and ankylosaurs.

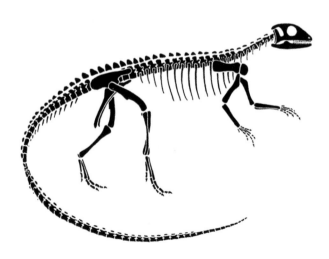

■ STEGOSAURUS

Age: Late Jurassic. **Fossils found:** western United States. **Size:** 30 feet long. **Features:** a stegosaur with two rows of upright triangular plates running from head to tail; two pairs of spikes on tail.

Stegosaurus was probably quadrupedal, although the hind legs were twice as long as the front legs. An obvious identifying feature of this distinctive dinosaur is the double row of erect, triangular plates on the back. The rest of the skeleton is quite similar to those of the more primitve ornithischians.

The spikes on the tail would appear to have been for protection. The function of the plates, however, is not obvious. The base of each plate was thickened, and seems to have been embedded in the animal's skin. The surfaces of the plates show fine grooves for blood vessels, indicating that both sides were covered with skin. This has led to speculation that the plates were used as heat-control devices. Ideas like this one are interesting, but cannot be substantiated because of the lack of evidence.

Other stegosaurs, *Kentrosaurus* from Africa and *Tuojiangosaurus* from China, have spines only or small plates and spines, suggesting that the armor is primarily defensive.

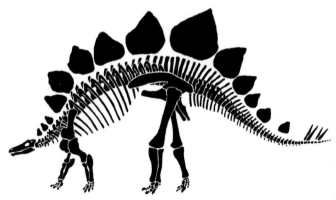

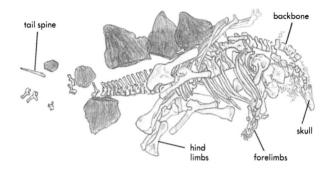

This outline of a *Stegosaurus* find shows the position of the bones as they were discovered. View is of the right side of the skeleton.

ANKYLOSAURIAN SKULLS

The skulls of ankylosaurs differ from those of other ornithischians in being very solid. In ankylosaurs, the skull openings characteristic of dinosaurs and other archosaurs are either quite restricted or are covered over by bone.

The front of the ankylosaurian skull is toothless, relatively large, and was probably covered with a large beak in both upper and lower jaws. In *Panoplosaurus* and its near relatives, it projects as a narrow beak. In *Euopocephalus* and more advanced ankylosaurs, it is much broader and bent downward. The cheek teeth, in a single row, are small and leaf-shaped, not very different from the primitive ornithischian condition but unusually small for the size of the skull. The teeth are set well back from the skull margins, producing a large cheek indentation.

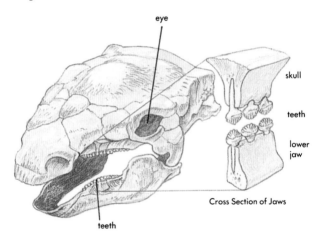

The small, single row of teeth in ankylosaurs contrasts strongly with the battery of thousands of teeth seen in ceratopsians and hadrosaurs.

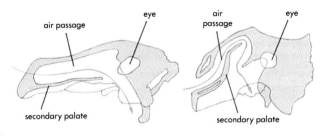

Panoplosaurus *Euoplocephalus*

Cross Section of Skulls

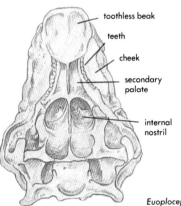

toothless beak

teeth

cheek

secondary palate

internal nostril

Bottom View of Skull

All ankylosaurs have a secondary palate that separates the air intake from food processing. *Panoplosaurus* had a relatively simple nasal chamber, but in *Euoplocephalus* and other advanced ankylosaurs, it developed into a bent passageway with complex associated sinuses of unknown function.

Euoplocephalus bony eyelid

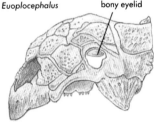

An interesting feature of the *Euoplocephalus* skull is the armored eyelid. Within the eye socket there were curved bony plates that presumably closed to cover the eyeball when needed.

107

EUOPLOCEPHALUS

Age: Late Cretaceous. **Fossils found:** western North America. **Size:** 22 feet long. **Features:** an ankylosaur; skull broad, with spikes at sides and back; large bony tail club.

Euoplocephalus is one of the best known of the ankylosaurs because partially articulated skeletons with skulls, armor, and limbs have been found. So far, however, there are no complete skeletons. *Euoplocephalus* had the "standard" ankylosaur body plan: it was a large quadrupedal animal covered with armor plates or knobs, its limbs were about equal in size, and its head and neck were short. Like other ankylosaurs and most dinosaurs, it apparently tucked its legs under its body, rather than sprawling. It could probably move quickly, at least at times, and was not necessarily slow and sluggish, depending entirely on its armor for defense.

Euoplocephalus and its near relatives differ from the nodosaurs in having a large tail club made up of enlarged ossicles fused to the tail vertebrae. (Nodosaurs lack a tail club.) The absence of a tail drag in trackways (p. 41) and the form of the bones indicate that the tail was held out and did not drag on the ground.

Ankylosaurus, a near relative of *Euoplocephalus*, is known from only a few partial specimens. Its estimated length of 35 feet makes it the largest ankylosaur.

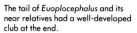

The tail of *Euoplocephalus* and its near relatives had a well-developed club at the end.

The tail of nodosaurs, such as *Sauropelta*, had no club.

EVOLUTION OF THE ORNITHOPOD DINOSAURS:
DUCK-BILLED DINOSAURS AND THEIR KIN

The ornithopods (which means "bird-footed," and refers to the three-toed hind feet) are a large group of ornithischian dinosaurs. Ornithopods include the duck-billed dinosaurs, or hadrosaurs, and their relatives—the iguanodonts, the camptosaurs, and the hypsilophodonts. All have similar skeletons, with differences occurring mainly in the skulls.

Duck-billed dinosaurs, or hadrosaurs, have a series of unique adaptations in the skull. But one of the most bizarre hadrosaur features is the enlargement of the nostrils to form huge nose openings and bony crests.

In *Hypsilophodon,* the nostril is the "normal" size and shape. In *Camptosaurus,* the snout is elongated and has a well-developed beak; the nostril is slightly enlarged. In *Iguanodon,* the beak and the nostril area are larger still. *Tenontosaurus* approaches the hadrosaur condition, with a nostril area that is about a third the length of the skull; there is a bulge between the eye and the nostril. In the hadrosaurs themselves (*Kritosaurus* and *Corythosaurus,* for example), we see the extreme condition: the nostril or nasal bones are more than half the length of the skull, and form a distinctive structure of some sort on top of the head.

There have been many speculations about the reasons for the evolution of these nasal structures, but this paleontological mystery—like so many others—may never be solved.

Facing page: The skulls of ornithopods developed complex expansions of the nasal area and nostrils (in orange). The culmination of these developments can be seen in the hadrosaurs, such as *Corythosaurus* and *Kritosaurus.* The functions of these enlargements are unknown.

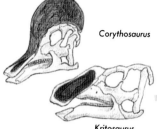

Corythosaurus

Hadrosaurs

Kritosaurus

Tenontosaurus

Iguanodon

Camptosaurus

Hypsilophodon

ANATOSAURUS

Age: Late Cretaceous. **Fossils found:** western North America. **Size:** 35 feet long. **Features:** ornithopod; a flat-headed hadrosaur with very elongate nose openings and without any bumps on the skull.

Anatosaurus is a well-known dinosaur, for, in addition to many good skeletons, two specimens with well-preserved skin imprints have been found. These two specimens, discovered by the Sternbergs, a family of professional fossil hunters, were probably formed by rapid burial in the mud and fine sand of a river system. The skin imprint in the sediment remained after the actual skin was gone.

After the first such specimens were found, it became apparent that some skin imprints were often preserved in dinosaurs from the Lance-Hell Creek fossil fields of Wyoming and the Belly River series of Alberta. One of these specimens has stomach contents preserved (p. 126).

The *Anatosaurus* skin impressions show that the animal was covered with scales that did not overlap, as they do in most lizards and snakes, but rather formed tubercles of various sizes. These were small, pointed tubercles forming a background with larger scales set into them.

Dinosaur "mummy," a skeleton of *Anatosaurus* from Wyoming that has skin impressions preserved

MAIASAURA

Age: Late Cretaceous. **Fossils found:** Montana. **Size:** 30 feet long. **Features:** ornithopod, similar to *Kritosaurus* but with a short, bony process extending forward between the eyes.

The discovery in 1978 by John Horner and Robert Makela of egg nests, hatchlings, juveniles, and adults of a new hadrosaur, *Maiasaura*, demonstrated that the fossil record continues to provide novelties even in such a well-prospected region as Montana. The association together, in one death assemblage, of nests, hatchlings, older juveniles, and adults suggested to Horner and Makela that the site was a nesting colony. They argued that the presence of older juveniles, about 3 feet long, meant that the hadrosaur young stayed under the care of the adults from the time they hatched until they became much older.

If Horner and Makela are correct, these hadrosaurs had a complex social organization, which some have said requires a mammalian physiology—that is, "warm-bloodedness." However, studies of recent crocodiles show that these "cold-blooded" relatives of dinosaurs also exhibit some degree of

parental care—guarding their young against predators by moving them to "nurseries," where they can be better protected. Again, we are faced with interesting ideas, but they are impossible to test rigorously.

This restoration of a *Maiasaura* nesting colony is based on the work of Horner on deposits near Choteau, Montana. This locality has yielded large mounds of soil that seem to have been made by hadrosaurs to hold eggs and possibly to have been used as "nurseries." Some of the juveniles may have been more than three years old before leaving the nest.

119

KRITOSAURUS

Age: Late Cretaceous. **Fossils found:** western North America. **Size:** 30 feet long. **Features:** ornithopod; a flat-headed hadrosaur with long nasal openings extending upward and ending in a prominent bump; otherwise similar to *Anatosaurus*.

Kritosaurus is known from a number of good specimens found in western Canada and southwestern United States. A medium-sized hadrosaur, or duck-billed dinosaur, it had a relatively deep and narrow skull with very long nasal openings, as in other non-crested hadrosaurs. In life, much of this space may have been filled with some kind of soft structure (p. 112). Folds of skin over most of the nasal openings in one of the *Anatosaurus* specimens with skin impressions support this idea. It has been speculated that a cartilaginous or even an inflatable sac fit over the nose in non-crested hadrosaurs and that this may have served the same function (whatever that was) as the crest in the crested hadrosaurs.

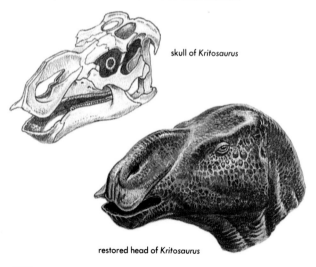

skull of *Kritosaurus*

restored head of *Kritosaurus*

SAUROLOPHUS

Age: Late Cretaceous. **Fossils found:** western North America and Asia. **Size:** 30 feet long. **Features:** ornithopod; a flat-headed hadrosaur with extremely long nasal openings and a solid bony spike extending up and back between the eyes and over the top of the skull.

Saurolophus had an elongated nasal surface forming what seems to have been the lower support for a larger nasal structure that was perhaps an inflatable or cartilaginous "balloon" (p. 112). *Saurolophus* was another of Barnum Brown's prizes during his work in the Red Deer River region of Alberta. A nearly complete skeleton was found associated with ripple marks and other evidence of stream burial. Does this mean that *Saurolophus* lived in rivers? Or was this hadrosaur only an occasional visitor to the riverbank? We only know that it was buried there and also buried relatively quickly because only a few bones are missing.

skull of *Saurolophus*

The skeleton preserved as it was found by Barnum Brown

LOCOMOTION IN DUCK-BILLED DINOSAURS

Duck-billed dinosaurs, or hadrosaurs, had hind limbs that were much longer and larger than the forelimbs, suggesting that they walked primarily on their hind legs. However, trackway evidence (p. 40) shows that at least at some times hadrosaurs walked on all fours and were quadrupedal. It is likely that they were quadrupedal when moving slowly, perhaps when feeding from the ground, but that they were bipedal when running or moving rapidly.

Hadrosaurs were apparently well adapted for running. The backbone in the area of the pelvis has a series of bony ligaments that crisscross each other and attach on the tops of the vertebrae. Present in all amniotes, these ligaments are usually made of flexible tissue, similar to rope. They become ossified, or bony, in only a few animals, and the result is a

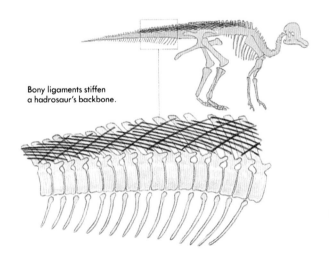

Bony ligaments stiffen
a hadrosaur's backbone.

Like other ornithopods, *Anatosaurus* was probably bipedal when running.

stiffening of the backbone so that it is only slightly flexible. This appears to be an adaptation for holding the backbone rigid during running, in a manner similar to such large flightless birds as the ostrich.

Specimens of hadrosaurs that preserve skin imprints give a somewhat different picture of hadrosaur locomotion, however. These specimens show that both the front and hind feet had webbing or skin between the fingers, a condition that is usually (but not necessarily) restricted to animals that use their limbs for swimming. It has also been argued, however, that the supposed webs were actually tough, fleshy pads used in dry land locomotion. On the other hand, a hadrosaur's tail was high and narrow, and could have been useful in swimming, which adds weight to the swimming theory.

The evidence seems somewhat contradictory, and again illustrates the serious limitations of trying to determine the behavior and biology of extinct animals. Hadrosaurs seem to have had adaptations for both dry land running and aquatic swimming, but were hadrosaurs necessarily restricted to one or the other?

125

FEEDING IN DUCK-BILLED DINOSAURS

In dinosaurs, the primitive tooth condition is a single row around the margins of the jaws. In hadrosaurs and other ornithischians, the teeth at the front of the jaws were lost and replaced with a horny beak. An increased number of teeth of greater complexity at the sides of the mouth resulted in the development of "batteries" of teeth in which each tooth position was occupied by thousands of teeth in various stages of growth and wear. The chewing surface was a formidable crushing and grinding mechanism.

Traditionally, hadrosaurs have been thought of as swamp-dwelling animals that fed on soft aquatic vegetation scooped up by means of the duck-billed snout. The jaw mechanism, however, appears to have been adapted for cutting and grinding some very tough plant material, quite different from soft water vegetation. One *Anatosaurus* specimen has pre-

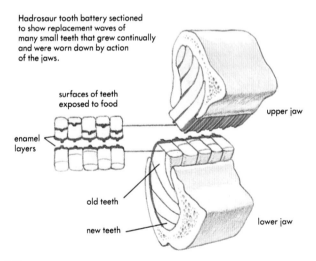

Hadrosaur tooth battery sectioned to show replacement waves of many small teeth that grew continually and were worn down by action of the jaws.

surfaces of teeth exposed to food

enamel layers

upper jaw

old teeth

new teeth

lower jaw

served stomach contents that consist of finely ground masses of plant material from evergreen trees. Needles, bark, and cone fragments are recognizable, and the ground-up condition of the material is consistent with the jaw mechanism. This is only one specimen, and it is possible that these stomach contents are quite different from the normal diet of hadrosaurs. It is a likely hypothesis, however, that our one sample is typical, and that at least some duck-billed dinosaurs fed on these plants.

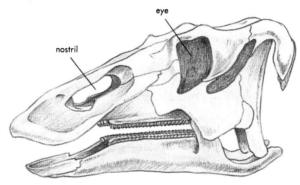

eye

nostril

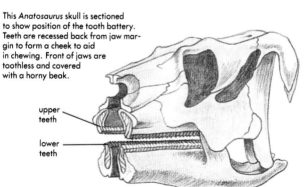

This *Anatosaurus* skull is sectioned to show position of the tooth battery. Teeth are recessed back from jaw margin to form a cheek to aid in chewing. Front of jaws are toothless and covered with a horny beak.

upper teeth

lower teeth

CRESTED HADROSAURS

The function of the grotesque bony outgrowths on the top of the skull in many hadrosaurs is a subject of speculation and unresolvable controversy. The crests are made up primarily of greatly elongated and expanded bones surrounding the nose and the nasal passages. These are bones that in other reptiles form short tubes containing the air passages. In a form like *Parasaurolophus*, the bony tubes extend over the top of the skull, then bend back underneath themselves to return to the skull. In others, like *Corythosaurus*, the bony passages form a large, hollow chamber on top of the skull. In some, like *Lambeosaurus*, some or all of the crest may have been solid. Flat-headed hadrosaurs also have nasal peculiarities, as the nasal opening itself is greatly expanded (pp. 120-121).

Once it was speculated that the crest might have served as a snorkel for the animal to breathe air while submerged with only the tip of its crest exposed. But the nasal opening is at the front of the skull rather than at the top. Comparably enlarged nasal areas in modern reptiles contain sensory tissue, and so perhaps the expanded nasal passages in these dinosaurs increased their ability to smell. A more imaginative speculation suggests that the different crest shapes produced different sounds, similar to whooping cranes, and that the sounds were related to courtship and to threat behavior. Despite the fact that hadrosaurs are one of the most well-preserved groups of extinct animals, the limitations of the fossil record do not allow objective choices to be made among these various speculations.

Facing page: These three hadrosaur skulls represent three types of nasal enlargements or crests seen in the group. *Parasaurolophus* has a tubular enlargement, *Lambeosaurus* a partially hollow, partially solid crest, and *Corythosaurus*, a completely hollow crest. The nasal passages are shown in blue.

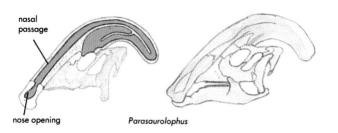

Parasaurolophus

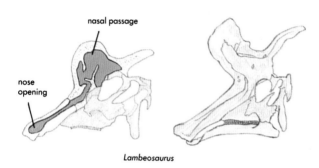

Lambeosaurus

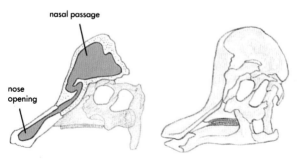

Corythosaurus

STEGOCERAS

Age: Late Cretaceous; near relatives from the Early Cretaceous. **Fossils found:** western North America; other pachycephalosaurs known from Asia, Africa, and Europe. **Size:** about 6½ feet long; *Pachycephalosaurus* was about 15 feet long. **Features:** bipedal pachycephalosaur; skull with thick bone but not dome-headed, as in *Pachycephalosaurus*; only small openings for eyes and jaw muscles.

Pachycephalosaurs, the bone-headed dinosaurs, are not as well known as most of the dinosaur groups. Some good skulls have been discovered, but postcranial bones are rare. *Stegoceras* is the only one known to date with adequate postcranial bones. Pachycephalosaurs had hind limbs much longer than the forelimbs and a long tail, similar to other ornithopods. They are presumed to have been bipedal. The skull, very different from other dinosaur skulls, was extremely thick on top and was surrounded by swollen tubercles along its edges. These enlarged back and side bones of the skull are similar to those of the horned dinosaurs, or ceratopsians, and indicate a close relationship between the two.

Stegoceras, 6 to 7 feet long, was less than half the size of *Pachycephalosaurus*.

It has been suggested that pachycephalosaurs used their thick skulls for butting against each other, but as usual with extinct animals, there is no compelling evidence in favor of this particular speculation.

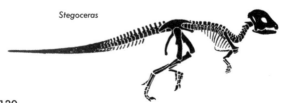

Stegoceras

brain cavity
(endocast)

Pachycephalosaurus is the largest known species in the group of bone-headed dinosaurs. It also had the thickest skull—a 10-inch layer of bone above the brain cavity. This sectioned skull shows the great thickness of bone on the top of the skull.

restoration of *Stegoceras*

SKULLS OF HORNED DINOSAURS

The prominent feature giving this group its name is the horn, but the expanded frill at the back of the skull is even more unusual.

Ceratopsians (horned dinosaurs) are related to pachycephalosaurs (bone-headed dinosaurs) because both groups have a shelf of enlarged bone at the back of the skull (p. 95). In the most primitive ceratopsian, *Psittacosaurus*, this shelf (purple in the illustration) is barely expanded. In more advanced ceratopsians, such as *Protoceratops* and *Triceratops*, it becomes very large—even larger than the rest of the skull. The frill is a better characteristic of horned dinosaurs than the horn, because the relatively primitive ceratopsians, such as *Protoceratops*, have frills but no horns.

A greatly expanded series of jaw muscles was attached to the frills. A characteristic of dinosaurs and all diapsids (p. 33) is two pairs of holes behind the eyes for jaw muscle attachments. In ceratopsians, the upper pair of these openings is expanded, the bone on the back border of the opening extending far beyond the rear of the skull. This expansion, or frill, took the muscles with it and presumably provided greater power or efficiency.

Advanced ceratopsians are usually divided into two groups: short-frilled, such as *Triceratops* (p. 144), and long-frilled, such as *Chasmosaurus* (p. 142). Most ceratopsians have a large opening in the center of the frill, but in *Triceratops*, this is closed, since the muscles were attached around the edge of the frill, and the presence or absence of this opening within the frill did not affect them.

Facing page: Evolution of frill (purple) from the most primitive ceratopsian, *Psittacosaurus*, to the relatively more advanced *Protoceratops*. Frill and horn development is even more advanced in later ceratopsians, such as *Triceratops*.

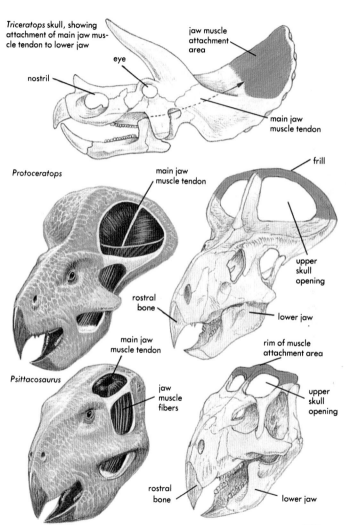

Triceratops skull, showing attachment of main jaw muscle tendon to lower jaw

jaw muscle attachment area

eye

nostril

main jaw muscle tendon

Protoceratops

main jaw muscle tendon

frill

rostral bone

upper skull opening

lower jaw

Psittacosaurus

main jaw muscle tendon

jaw muscle fibers

rim of muscle attachment area

upper skull opening

rostral bone

lower jaw

133

FEEDING IN HORNED DINOSAURS

The most primitive horned dinosaurs had a single row of teeth, similar to that seen in primitive ornithopods. As shown in the ornithischian family tree (pp. 94-95), the teeth of the horned dinosaurs had thicker enamel on one side of the tooth (a cerapod character), and the teeth were recessed to form a cheek (a genasaurian character). Because each individual tooth had thicker enamel on one side, it wore down more slowly than the other side and produced a sharp edge.

In *Triceratops* and other advanced ceratopsians, the number of teeth and the length of the tooth row was greatly increased in comparison to the relatively more primitive *Protoceratops*. Duck-billed dinosaurs, or hadrosaurs, had tooth batteries similar to those of the ceratopsians, but both groups evolved these batteries independently and apparently for different purposes. In hadrosaurs, the chewing surface was a rough, rasplike surface that met the opposing surface directly. In the ceratopsians, the flat surfaces of the teeth did

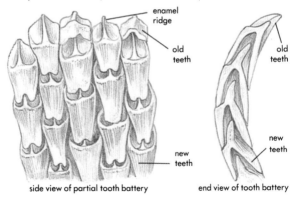

side view of partial tooth battery   end view of tooth battery

Ceratopsian teeth were arranged in dense groups, or batteries. This produced an ever-growing and constantly sharp surface that could slice and cut tough plant material.

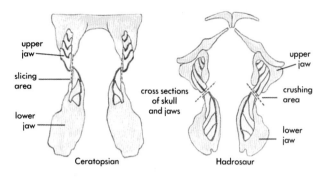

Tooth batteries of ceratopsians (left) were arranged as vertical surfaces that could slice food. In hadrosaurs (right) the batteries were oriented for grinding and crushing.

not meet directly, but slid past each other. Duckbills apparently crushed and mashed food while the ceratopsians sliced their food. The teeth batteries of both were capable of dealing with very tough vegetation, but of different types. Duckbills are known to have eaten evergreen needles, cones, and bark (p. 126). We can only guess that ceratopsians may have fed on cycads and other similar, fibrous plants.

Lower jaws of ceratopsians, with teeth exposed. Relatively more primitive *Protoceratops* had some teeth close together, but the more advanced *Triceratops* had many more teeth concentrated into a dental battery.

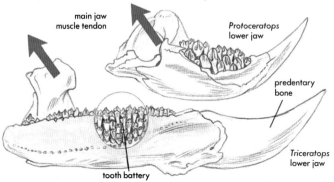

PROTOCERATOPS

Age: Late Cretaceous. **Fossils found:** Mongolia; close relatives in North America. **Size:** 6 feet long. **Features:** a small ceratopsian with a frill but without horns.

Protoceratops has the expanded frill (p. 132) of the horned dinosaurs that are advanced over *Psittacosaurus*. It also has the ceratopsian feature of an extra bone, the rostral bone (p. 133), at the front of the skull, but it did not have horns on the skull. Dozens of skulls, partial skeletons, and a number of complete skeletons of this primitive horned dinosaur were collected on American Museum of Natural History expeditions to Mongolia in the 1920s. Enough skulls were found to put together one of the few growth series available for dinosaurs.

The most famous single result of the work in Mongolia was the discovery of dinosaur eggs. Fragments of eggs had been known earlier, but for the first time whole nests of eggs associated with one particular dinosaur were found. Juveniles and hatchlings were also discovered. Although the expedition collected other dinosaurs and the scientifically more important Cretaceous mammal skulls and turtles, the dinosaur eggs became the event most closely linked with the Mongolian work.

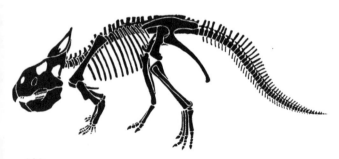

Above left: Roy Chapman Andrews, expedition leader, with a nest of *Protoceratops* eggs in Mongolia in 1925. Right: *Protoceratops* egg nest showing orientaton of the eggs, with long axis pointing to center. The eggs were preserved in wind-blown sand that apparently covered the nest so deeply the babies couldn't hatch.

STYRACOSAURUS

Age: Late Cretaceous. **Fossils found:** western North America. **Size:** 18 feet long. **Features:** large, short-frilled ceratopsian with a long nose horn, no brow horns, and six large spikes around the edge of the frill.

Styracosaurus is one of the more bizarre of the horned dinosaurs. Its short frill with large openings had three pairs of spikes around the edge. The spikes suggest there might have been some protective function for the frill.

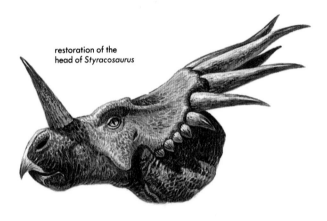

restoration of the head of *Styracosaurus*

American Museum of Natural History skeleton of *Styracosaurus*. See p. 19 for photo of this skeleton being mounted.

PACHYRHINOSAURUS

Age: Late Cretaceous. **Fossils found:** Alberta and Alaska. **Size:** probably 15 to 18 feet long. **Features:** short-frilled ceratopsian with no facial horns but a very thick, flat area on the nose between the eyes.

Pachyrhinosaurus is still imperfectly known, and the skull shown here is a reconstruction based on incomplete specimens. Except for the skull, little is known of the rest of the skeleton. The thick, roughened area of bone on the skull seems to have been a surface that would allow butting of some sort. But as with all ideas about the behavior of extinct animals, the function of the roughened area in *Pachyrhinosaurus* cannot be determined. Recently, *Pachyrhinosaurus* has been found in Alaska, a region that hadn't yielded dinosaurs in the past. In addition to adult specimens, smaller specimens were found that are presumably juveniles.

CHASMOSAURUS

Age: Late Cretaceous. **Fossils found:** western North America. **Size:** 17 feet long. **Features:** long-frilled ceratopsian with two large brow horns and a small nose horn; frill with a "window" and without spikes.

Chasmosaurus had a very long frill formed by a relatively thin, bony framework quite distinct from the short frill of *Monoclonius* and the solid frill of *Triceratops* (p. 144). A frill of this sort could scarcely have provided much protection and supports the idea of the frill as muscle attachment. It has been speculated, however, that the horns and frill were primarily for display.

MONOCLONIUS

Age: Late Cretaceous. **Fossils found:** western North America. **Size:** 20 feet long. **Features:** short-frilled ceratopsian with a large nose horn, very small brow horns; frill with a "window" and without spikes.

Monoclonius (possibly the same genus as *Centrosaurus*) is one of the best-known horned dinosaurs. It is represented by a nearly complete skeleton from Alberta on exhibit in the American Museum of Natural History in New York (p. 19). This horned dinosaur is one of the short-frilled species and is distinguished by a single large horn on the nose. In some specimens the nose horn is sharply curved forward. Why this is so is not known.

143

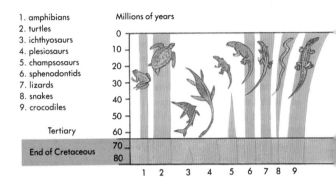

	Millions of years	
1. amphibians	0	
2. turtles	10	
3. ichthyosaurs	20	
4. plesiosaurs	30	
5. champsosaurs	40	
6. sphenodontids	50	
7. lizards	60	
8. snakes	70	
9. crocodiles	80	

Tertiary — 60

End of Cretaceous — 70–80

1 2 3 4 5 6 7 8 9

THE END OF THE DINOSAURS

One of the great fascinations of dinosaurs is the mystery of their extinction (although we would now say that they are not extinct, because birds are dinosaurs). Dozens of theories have been proposed to explain their end; which, if any, are true?

It is necessary to see which theories are testable and which are just speculation. One fact cannot be emphasized enough: the fossil record is very fragmentary. Most of the information necessary to scientifically criticize and test ideas about extinction is not even preserved in the fossil record.

First of all, the geologically youngest dinosaur skeletons that can definitely be dated are about 65 million years old, from the Late Cretaceous. However, there may be errors of up to 10 million years in correlating the youngest dinosaurs from different continents. As a result of intensive work over the past few years, more evidence is accumulating that shows that dinosaur species had been declining over about 20 million years before the end of the Cretaceous.

10. pterosaurs
11. theropods
    (except birds)
12. sauropods
13. ornithopods
14. stegosaurs
15. armored dinosaurs
16. horned dinosaurs
17. birds
18. mammals

10 11 12 13 14 15 16 17 18

Secondly, many different kinds of living things were also extinct by the end of the Cretaceous. The pterosaurs (flying reptiles), mosasaurs, plesiosaurs, and ichthyosaurs (marine reptiles related to lizards and snakes) also became extinct. But none of these groups were dinosaurs. Among other groups of living things that were extinct by the end of the Cretaceous period are groups of one-celled organisms and some mollusk groups. The fossil record is not exact enough to determine precisely when all these groups became extinct.

A third important fact about dinosaur extinction is that they did not really become extinct. As discussed earlier (see p. 92), birds are dinosaurs, and they survived the Cretaceous to become prominent forms of life living today. So it is incorrect to say that dinosaurs became extinct in the first place.

To summarize what we know: 1. most dinosaurs (except birds) became extinct about 65 million years ago, although many probably became extinct earlier; 2. many other groups of animals also became extinct at approximately the same time; and 3. some dinosaurs survived—namely, birds.

EVOLUTION OF THE MAMMALS

Mammals are four-footed animals that have hair and suckle their young with milk secreted by glands. Cows, dogs, monkeys, and humans are mammals. After all the dinosaurs except birds became extinct, the mammals occupied the habitats left by the dinosaurs. But the mammals did not cause or contribute to the extinction of the dinosaurs. Mammals belong to a group called synapsids (p. 33) that also includes their extinct relatives. Synapsids evolved long before dinosaurs and are characterized by a single opening in the skull

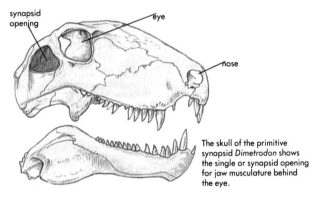

synapsid opening

eye

nose

The skull of the primitive synapsid *Dimetrodon* shows the single or synapsid opening for jaw musculature behind the eye.

Stages in the Evolution of Mammals

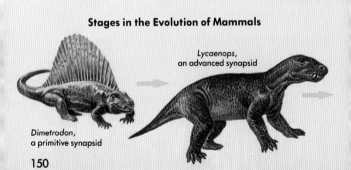

Lycaenops,
an advanced synapsid

Dimetrodon,
a primitive synapsid

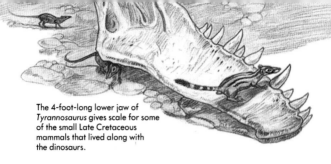

The 4-foot-long lower jaw of *Tyrannosaurus* gives scale for some of the small Late Cretaceous mammals that lived along with the dinosaurs.

behind the eye. The first mammals evolved from primitive synapsids like *Dimetrodon*, and appeared at about the same time as dinosaurs.

For millions of years the mammals remained relatively stable, although their basic diversification took place before dinosaurs became extinct. Many millions of years passed before the apes evolved, and close relatives of humans do not appear in the fossil record until about 3 million years ago, more than 60 million years after the dinosaurs became extinct.

Why did birds and mammals survive and so many other groups become extinct? No one knows, but it is a question that is constantly asked, and one that may be impossible for us ever to answer.

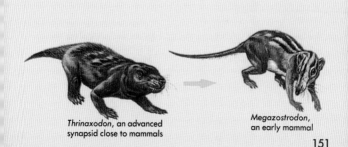

Thrinaxodon, an advanced synapsid close to mammals

Megazostrodon, an early mammal

151

CAREER OPPORTUNITIES IN PALEONTOLOGY

Paleontology is the study of fossils—any fossils, plants or animals. Vertebrate paleontology is the study of the fossils of animals with backbones, including dinosaurs.

Professional vertebrate paleontologists in North America usually work for museums or universities, and are responsible for collections, teaching, exhibitions, and research.

Most paleontologists concentrate on a particular group of animals and also adopt a particular point of view or approach to their study. They may concern themselves with the diversity and evolutionary relationships of the animals they study. If so, they are systematists. Systematists must really be anatomists and study related living animals as

Building an exhibit

Teaching

well as extinct ones. In addition to studying animal diversity, paleontologists may concentrate on more geologic problems and study the age of fossils or their stratigraphy. Or they may study zoogeography, which concerns the distribution of animals. Anatomical studies of fossils often lead to attempts to determine the mechanics of the bones or their functional morphology.

Most people think that paleontologists spend a great deal of their time in the field. Usually only a small portion of time is taken up by field work. University or museum responsibilities take time, but the greatest limit to field work is the money available to maintain it.

In field work, something exciting may be found in the first month or two, but it may then take three or four years to prepare and describe the find.

In order to become a vertebrate paleontologist, get the highest grades possible and go to the best schools you can. As an undergraduate, a biology or geology major would be preferred. If a student has the choice between a top science school without a vertebrate paleontologist on the faculty and a less satisfactory but still good school with a paleontologist, definitely go to the better school. When choosing a graduate school, more care must be taken to find a strong program, preferably with more than one vertebrate paleontologist and a good collection. Probably only

Making field notes and sketches

about half of the vertebrate paleontologist PhD graduates of North American universities get the kind of job they want. A lot depends upon luck at this stage; good positions do not become available very often.

Paleontology, if it is to be a worthwhile scientific endeavor, requires just as much tedious and frustrating effort as any other important occupation. But it does have some wonderful moments.

Digging in the field

DINOSAUR DISPLAYS

Major Dinosaur Exhibitions of North America

Academy of Natural Sciences
19th and the Parkway
Logan Square
Philadelphia, Pennsylvania
  19103

American Museum of Natural
  History
Central Park West and
  79th Street
New York, New York 10024

Carnegie Museum of Natural
  History
4400 Forbes Avenue
Pittsburgh, Pennsylvania
  15213

Field Museum of Natural
  History
Roosevelt Road at Lake
  Shore Drive
Chicago, Illinois 60605

Los Angeles County Museum
900 Exposition Boulevard
Los Angeles, California 90007

National Museum of Natural
  History
Smithsonian Institution
Washington, D.C. 20560

National Museum of Natural
  Sciences
P.O. 3443
Station D
Ottawa K1P6P4, Canada

Peabody Museum of Natural
  History
Yale University
170 Whitney Avenue
New Haven, Connecticut 06511

Royal Ontario Museum
100 Queen's Park
Toronto, Ontario M5S2C6
Canada

Tyrrell Museum of Palaeontology
P.O. Box 7500
Drumheller, Alberta T0J0Y0
Canada

The American Museum of Natural History, listed above, is the world's largest and most representative collection and exhibition of dinosaurs. A special reference must be made to Dinosaur National Monument, P.O. Box 128, Jensen, Utah 84035. This is the largest "in place" exhibition of dinosaur bones, with nearly 2,000 bones shown in the rock. Other "in place" exhibits are Dinosaur Provincial Park, Patricia, Alberta, and Rocky Hill Dinosaur State Park, Rocky Hill, Connecticut (trackways of Triassic dinosaurs).

Other Museums With Dinosaur Displays

Buffalo Museum of Science
1020 Humboldt Parkway
Buffalo, New York 14211

Museum of Northern Arizona
Route 4, Box 720
Flagstaff, Arizona 86001

154

Quarry wall at Dinosaur National Monument

Cleveland Museum of Natural
    History
Wade Oval
Cleveland, Ohio 44106

Denver Museum of Natural History
City Park
Denver, Colorado 80205

Earth Sciences Museum
Brigham Young University
Provo, Utah 84602

Forth Worth Museum of Science
1501 Montgomery Street
Forth Worth, Texas 76107

Geological Museum
University of Wyoming
Laramie, Wyoming 82071

Houston Museum of Natural
    Science
1 Hermann Circle Drive
Houston, Texas 77030

Museum of Comparative Zoology
Harvard University
Cambridge, Massachusetts
    02138

Museum of Paleontology
University of California
Berkeley, California 94720

Museum of the Rockies
Montana State University
Bozeman, Montana 59715

Pratt Museum
Amherst College
Amherst, Massachusetts 01002

Redpath Museum
McGill University
859 Sherbrook Street West
Montreal, Quebec H3A2K6,
Canada

Ruthven Museum
University of Michigan
Ann Arbor, Michigan 48109

Utah Museum of Natural
    History
University of Utah
Salt Lake City, Utah 84112

MORE INFORMATION

Best Single Source on Dinosaurs

Norman, D. *Illustrated Encyclopedia of Dinosaurs*. New York: Outlet Book Co., 1985.

Highly Recommended Popular Books

British Museum of Natural History. *Dinosaurs and Their Living Relatives,* 2nd ed. New York: Cambridge University Press, 1986.

Colbert, Edwin H. *Dinosaurs: An Illustrated History*. Maplewood, New Jersey: Hammond, Inc., 1983.

Lambert, D. *A Field Guide to Dinosaurs*. New York: Avon Books, 1983.

Other Useful Popular Books

Charig, Alan J. *A New Look at the Dinosaurs*. New York: Facts on File, 1983.

Colbert, E. H. *Dinosaurs: Their Discovery and Their World*. New York: E. P. Dutton and Co., 1964.

Halstead, L. B., and Jenny Halstead. *Dinosaurs*. New York: Sterling Publishing Co., 1987.

Russell, Dale A. *A Vanished World: The Dinosaurs of Western Canada*. Ottawa: National Museum of Canada, 1977.

Sattler, Helen R. *Dinosaurs of North America*. New York: Lothrop, Lee & Shepard Books, 1981.

Stout, W. *The Dinosaurs*. New York: Bantam Books, 1981. Interesting figures, text often speculative.

Wilford, John N. *The Riddle of the Dinosaur*. New York: Random House, 1987.

Books for Younger Readers

Norman, D. *When Dinosaurs Ruled the Earth*. New York: Exeter, 1985.

Robinson, H. R., ed. *Ranger Rick's Dinosaur Book*. Vienna, Virginia: National Wildlife Federation, 1984.

Collecting Dinosaurs

Bird, Roland T. *Bones for Barnum Brown: Adventures of a Dinosaur Hunter*. Forth Worth: Texas Christian University Press, 1985.

Colbert, E. H. *Men and Dinosaurs: The Search in Field and Laboratory.* New York: E. P. Dutton and Co., 1968. The best history of dinosaur collecting.

Kielan-Jaworowska, Z. *Hunting for Dinosaurs.* Cambridge: MIT Press, 1969. Collecting dinosaurs in Mongolia.

Sternberg, Charles H. *Hunting Dinosaurs in the Badlands of the Red Deer River, Alberta, Canada.* Lawrence, Kansas: The World Company Press, 1909. Both this book and the one below are classic narratives of fossil collecting in the "golden age."

Sternberg, Charles H. *The Life of a Fossil Hunter.* New York: Henry Holt & Co., 1909. Hard to find.

Technical References of More General Interest

Gauthier, J.A. "Saurischian Monophyly and the Origin of Birds." In *The Origin of Birds and the Evolution of Flight* (ed. K. Padian), Memoirs of the California Academy of Science, Vol. 8 (1986), pp. 1-55.

Romer, Alfred S. *Osteology of the Reptiles.* Chicago: University of Chicago Press, 1976.

Sereno, P. C. "Phylogeny of the Bird-hipped Dinosaurs (Order Ornithischia)." *National Geographic Research,* Vol. 2, No. 2 (1986), pp. 234-256.

Related Fields

Carroll, Robert L. *Vertebrate Paleontology and Evolution.* New York: W. H. Freeman, 1987.

Eldredge, Niles, and Joel Cracraft. *Phylogenetic Patterns and the Evolutionary Process.* New York: Columbia University Press, 1984.

Eldredge, Niles, and Ian Tattersall. *The Myths of Human Evolution.* New York: Columbia University Press, 1982.

Patterson, Colin. *Evolution.* Ithaca: Cornell University Press, 1978.

Rhodes, Frank H. T., Herbert Zim, and Paul Shaffer. *Fossils.* New York: Golden Press, 1962.

The *Journal of Vertebrate Paleontology,* published by the Society of Vertebrate Paleontology, often includes papers on dinosaurs. The Society has memberships for serious amateurs and yearly meetings with field trips and talks. For information, contact the paleontology department of a major museum or university.

INDEX

Numbers in **boldface** indicate the page or pages
where a dinosaur is described and illustrated.

PHOTO CREDITS

The following photographs are reproduced Courtesy Department of Library Services, American Museum of Natural History: p. 19 top, Neg. no. 315117; p. 19 middle, Neg. no. 36216; p. 19 bottom, Neg. no. 36214; p. 71, Neg. no. 2A2786; p. 76, Transparency no. 2418; p. 77 top, Neg. no. 35422; p. 77 bottom, Neg. no. 28039; p. 116, Neg. no. 330491, photo by A.E. Anderson; p. 121, Neg. no. 324069; p. 122 top, Neg. no. 324088; p. 122 bottom, Neg. no. 324068; p. 123 top, Neg. no. 324087; p. 139 top left, Neg. no. 410743; p. 139 top right, Neg. no. 324083; p. 140, Neg. no. 315309. The photograph on p. 91 is by the author.